Overcoming Abuse: Embracing Peace. What a treasure-trove of help and hope! This author tackles one of the toughest topics on Earth—the tragedy of abuse. Davison knows that most people throughout the world are ignorant about the why's of abuse and especially the what-to-do's.

The pervasiveness of domestic violence is appalling (1 in 3 women worldwide). The *prevalence of childhood sexual abuse is heartbreaking—we must intervene.*

Thankfully, these insightful pages are filled with a plethora of Scriptural principles and *practical strategies ready for us to apply—to set the captives free. Consequently, to help us and to help us help others, we all need these books.*

June Hunt
Broadcaster, Hope for the Heart
Author, *Counseling Through Your Bible Handbook*

Reina Davison provides essential hope to abuse victims and valuable guidance to those who counsel and care for them. Overcoming Abuse Embracing Peace Volume I, II, and III are unique contributions to the understanding and treatment of abuse trauma. These are must have tools for counselors, caregivers, and abuse sufferers alike.

Major General Bob Dees, U.S. Army, Retired
Author, *The Resilience Trilogy and Resilience God Style*

As the author of *When Your Husband is Addicted to Pornography: Healing Your Wounded Heart*, I frequently receive communication from pastors, ministry leaders, family members, and others who care about women who find themselves in abusive situations. Typically, they feel ill-equipped to help; lacking resources and words which will promote healing rather than causing more pain. *Overcoming Abuse Volume III* is a valuable resource for those who care to help.

Vicki Tiede
Vicki Tiede Ministries
Certified Health Coach

If women and children are ever to count as equals with men -- and abuse is one of the pivotal matters --, the change must come about in our time. With this in mind, Reina Davison's *Overcoming Abuse: Embracing Peace* Volume I, II, and III strike us as a compassionate enterprise of the first importance. May it flourish for years to come.

Julia O'Faolain, Novelist
Lauro Martines, Historian

The subtitles for Reina Davison's books are not exaggerations. The word 'encyclopedic' is accurate. These *Overcoming Abuse* companion volumes I, II, and III provide helpers and victims alike with a wealth of important insights into the tragic problem of abusive relationships and how to deal with them.

Abuse is a difficult problem for churches and church leaders to address. In the first place, abuse is not as simple as it might seem to the casual observer. It is complex, secretive, and entrenched. Simple exhortations or solutions do little more than allow the abuse to continue. Second, while abuse has significant spiritual causes, the role of psychological and emotional factors requires deeper and more nuanced understanding. Abuse is not a problem for mere spiritual formation strategies. It requires a comprehensive and professional set of interventions before it will give way to peace and freedom for the victim. Third, the church has a long history of male-dominated leadership. One of the most tragic consequences of this gender imbalance is that well-intentioned 'helpers' in the church often give more credence to the reports of males than to the plaints of women. Too often the church blames the victim for the abuse without taking into consideration the entire scope of the issues involved.

These books contain first-person accounts of victims that grip your heart. The tragedy that these victims have endured is immense. Yet we can all learn by listening to their stories and taking their experiences seriously. The massive problem of abuse in relationships, even those within the church, require all of us to be informed and equipped to deal effectively with it. The Overcoming Abuse volumes go a long way to do just that.

James R. Beck, Ph.D.
Senior Professor of Counseling
Denver Seminary

Overcoming Abuse Embracing Peace

VOLUME III

AN ENCYCLOPEDIC GUIDE FOR
HELPERS OF ABUSE VICTIMS

Reina Davison

NEW HARBOR PRESS
Rapid City, SD

Copyright © 2020 by Reina Davison.

All rights reserved. No part of this publication may be reproduced, distributed or transmitted in any form or by any means, including photocopying, recording, or other electronic or mechanical methods, without the prior written permission of the publisher, except in the case of brief quotations embodied in critical reviews and certain other noncommercial uses permitted by copyright law. For permission requests, write to the publisher, addressed "Attention: Permissions Coordinator," at the address below.

Davison/New Harbor Press
1601 Mt. Rushmore Rd., Ste 3288
Rapid City, SD 57701
www.NewHarborPress.com

Ordering Information:
Quantity sales. Special discounts are available on quantity purchases by corporations, associations, and others. For details, contact the "Special Sales Department" at the address above.

Overcoming Abuse Embracing Peace Vol III/Reina Davison. —1st ed.
ISBN 978-1-63357-317-8

Cover art by Victoria Aleice
Author photo by Tessa Klingensmith

This book is a work of non-fiction. Unless otherwise noted, the author and the publisher make no explicit guarantees as to the accuracy of the information contained in this book and in some cases, names of people and places have been altered to protect their privacy. The information, ideas, and suggestions in this book are not intended as a substitute for professional advice. Before following any suggestions contained in this book, you should consult your personal physician or mental health professional. Neither the author nor the publisher shall be liable or responsible for any loss or damage allegedly arising as a consequence of your use or application of any information or suggestions in this book. Because of the dynamic nature of the Internet, any web addresses or links contained in this book may have changed since publication and may no longer be valid.

The author has researched data and sources which are believed to be reliable information that is in accordance with the professional code of ethics and current standards of practice at the time of publication. In the event of the possibility of human error or changes in the medical and mental health sciences, neither the author nor the editor and publisher, or any other parties who were involved in the process or publication of this book guarantees that the information contained in this work is complete and flawless in respect to accuracy and they are not responsible for accidental omissions, errors, or any outcomes which result from the use of the information in this book. Readers are encouraged to consult with Scripture, continue the research contained in this book, and to confirm with additional sources.

All Scripture quotations are taken from the New King James Version®. Copyright 1982 by Thomas Nelson, Inc. Used by permission. All rights reserved.

Dedicated to all lay persons and those in the helping professions who have served and continue to serve victims of abuse.

Pure and undefiled religion before God and the Father is this: to visit orphans and widows in their trouble, and to keep oneself unspotted from the world.

- James 1:27 -

Contents

FOREWORD 1

ACKNOWLEDGMENTS 5

NOTE ON SELECTED TERMINOLOGY 9

THE PURPOSE OF THESE BOOKS 15

PART I

AMERICA'S HISTORY OF ABUSE 21

    Women as Men's Property 21

    Sin as the Origin of Abuse 23

    Religion and Women as Property 26

    Historical View of Women Must Change 30

SUZANNE'S STORY 41

PART II

RECONCILIATION ADVISOR VS.
THE PROFESSIONAL 51

    The Reconciliation Advisor (R.A.) 51

    Professionals Prioritize Safety 66

    Establishing a Safety Escape Plan
    with the Victim 71

Establishing a Post-Escape Plan
with the *Overcomer*.. 82

Helping the Victim with the Here & Now 86

Helping the Victim Process Safety Decisions........................ 87

Role Modeling a Balance of
Trust & Self-Protection.. 90

Providing Support When the Victim Regresses.................... 95

Cognitive Behavioral Therapy (CBT) &
Reality Therapy (RT).. 100

A Family Systems Approach to
Restoration of Identity... 104

A Neurological Approach to Victim Trauma 107

Attachment & Brain Dominance 113

Combining CBT, Reality Therapy, & Neurology 128

Post-Traumatic Stress Disorder (PTSD) 129

Treating PTSD with Exposure Therapy 136

PTSD Prognosis for the *Overcomer* 140

Group Therapy.. 141

Christian Counseling 145

The Spirit, Mind, and Body 156

How Can a Victim Become an *Overcomer*? 163

Helping to Heal & Stop
the Trauma of Victim Abuse.. 169

HANNAH'S STORY 179

PART III
HELPERS AND SOCIETY CAN OVERCOME ABUSE 191

Victim & Society Redemption 191

What can a Lay Person do When Abuse is Suspected? 200

Domestic Violence in the Military—How Can You Help? 206

How to Help a Victim of Digital Abuse 210

Victim Abuse can be Overcome one Victim at a Time 217

LIZ'S STORY 223

ENDNOTES 233

RESOURCES 235

WOMAN ABUSE SCREENING TOOL (WAST) 241

Adult Victim Domestic Violence Assessment Tool 242

SAMPLE TECHNOLOGY ABUSE LOG 244

Using the HELPS Tool with Women Seeking Domestic Violence Services 245

HELPS Screening Tool for Traumatic Brain Injury 247

OTHER BOOKS BY REINA DAVISON 249

FOREWORD

When Reina Davison initially asked me to provide a Foreword for the *Overcoming Abuse* book series, I was flattered, to be sure, but I did wonder quietly what our respective professions had in common, and how I could best introduce a book on a subject matter with which I was, mercifully, not terribly familiar. My career, after all, has been in the realm of clinical medicine, as a practitioner of Critical Care. For the better part of four decades, my days have been spent at the bedsides of the critically ill and dying in the intensive care unit of military and civilian hospitals. These patients are terribly ill, deeply broken physically and emotionally, and yes, spiritually. In many cases, their illness has befallen them because of inadvisable choices they have made in their lives; in others, illness has come unbidden, if you will, seemingly at random. Regardless, the devastation of their affliction is great, and their suffering, unknowable.

But clinically, I have not been acquainted with victims of abuse—or have I? Of course, I knew a few victims...a friend or a relative, one in particular, now long deceased (by suicide), about whose "situation" my mom had told me. And, "situations," as we called many things back then, were not openly discussed. Isn't that the case for many of us—we know *about* someone who is a victim of abuse, but not much more.

But Davison reassured me...she had heard me lecture on things medical through a spiritual lens; we have this much in common, that we trust in a Lord who is acquainted with grief and suffering, *our* grief and suffering, into which He entered, and enters, completely, and in which He is present to meet us and to be, finally, the only Source of healing and restoration.

Thus encouraged, I read the manuscripts—and it didn't take long before several dimensions of this work began to stand out. The first of these is Davison's breadth and depth of experience as a counselor and friend to the victims of abuse. She is a keen clinician, one who speaks authoritatively on her field of practice. She is knowledgeable in the subject of abuse, perceptive of the nuances of the illness, and familiar with pertinent literature on the subject. Like an astute physician, she is not fooled by the nuances of victims' symptoms, nor by the subconsciously illusive turns of the history that the abused will give, nor by the psychopathology of the abuser. Nor by the shroud of, well, frank *ignorance and denial* of abuse, which is individually and societally symptomatic of the disease itself and of its deep evil.

So it began to dawn on me that her line of work is not terribly divergent, after all, from my own. Victims of abuse are critically ill, and desperately so, and in need of their own form of *intensive care*. Davison provides precisely that: care for the victim and a resource for those who would care for them. And, like any great advocate, she is an educator—not only of the victim and their counselors, but of her readers. These books are nothing short of revelatory for those of us who, hitherto, "may only have known about" a victim, whether because we did not know the signs or manifestations, or because these were "situations" about which one doesn't speak. Perhaps *I have* met a number of

FOREWORD

people—friend, relative, or patient—who have been victims, secretly suffering, and I never knew, because I hadn't been aware. These books raise consciousness.

The second dimension that caught my eye was Davison's faithfulness to the biblical teaching of the redemptive work of Christ and of the active and very real presence of the Holy Spirit to heal and restore. Davison's text is punctuated with the personal accounts of victims. Their path to healing is never "fake," as in the well caricatured tossing away of a no-longer-needed set of crutches, but of the complex, often tedious, but fundamentally important healing process that occurs over time and as a result of sound therapy, patience, and much prayer. The Holy Spirit is no less present and active in these long and difficult processes than in the dramatic healing of the paralytic at the Beautiful Gate (Acts 3:1-10). Davison's is not an appeal to a vague secular "spirituality," but to the mighty Triune God. The hope she offers is rock-solid.

The third key dimension of these books for me is their inherent and urgent relevance for the Church. It has always been incumbent upon the Church universal and the Church local to be sensitive and responsive to the deep brokenness of her members. Inasmuch as the Apostle Paul understands the institution of marriage itself to be the visible symbol of Christ and His church (Ephesians 5:32), we see perhaps no greater consequence of the fall of humankind than abuse, marital discord, dysfunction, and rupture. But do some churches strain to keep a marriage intact at the expense of the well-being or even the life of a victim of abuse? Davison is not shy to address this head-on. If the recognition, diagnosis, intervention, and counsel of abuse victims are not on the heart and in the pastoral care ministry of a church, then that church has work to do. Davison's books should find their way onto every pastor's desk, and into seminary curricula.

Ministry to victim and to abuser, like medical treatment of critically ill patients, is not for the faint of heart. Ministry and treatment are all about the rolling up of the sleeves of our hearts and minds, the speaking openly about the unspeakable, and entering into the thick darkness of compassion as we come alongside victims and abusers in the hard work of redemption, remembering, all the while, that thick darkness is the very place where God Himself is known to dwell. The prayers of the afflicted do certainly rise to the throne of God. Reina Davison has given practical wisdom of life and hope to those who are in deep and abiding need.

Allen H. Roberts II, M.D., M.Div., M.A. (Bioethics)
Professor of Clinical Medicine
Georgetown University Medical Center

ACKNOWLEDGMENTS

A HEARTFELT THANK YOU to the abusers and victims of whom these books are written; it is regrettable that there had to be abusers and victims for these books to be written, but the hope is that out of these tragic abusive relationships, victims will be reached and many lives will be saved. A wholehearted thank you to each Overcomer for responding in a humanitarian way by pouring out your heart and allowing your story to be shared in these books.

Thank you, colleagues—too many to acknowledge, but you know who you are because you sacrificially gave of your time to disclose your professional experiences in the community, with the government, the judicial system, with abusers and the victims of abuse.

Thank you, Hershall Seals, for taking time out of your schedule on some beautiful summer days and actually painting alongside Victoria Aleice on your own canvas as she created the covers for Volume I, II, and III, of the *Overcoming Abuse: Embracing Peace* book series. Thank you, Victoria Aleice, for painting the book covers with the exact vision I proposed to you; an oil painting with purple clouds (as purple is the official color for domestic violence awareness) depicting the darkness of the trauma of abuse on the bottom which then flows into an ombre lavender, fading into white clouds and sun (SON) rays streaming down at the top to represent the healing from darkness (abuse victim trauma) that turns into light (an Overcomer light of Christ).

Thank you, Dr. Roberts, for taking time out of your busy life to meticulously research and read the manuscripts for the *Overcoming Abuse: Embracing Peace* book series, and then writing a foreword. Thank you for caring about this ministry medically, educationally, and spiritually.

Thank you, Mary Ellis Rice, for poring over the *Overcoming Abuse: Embracing Peace* manuscripts and for proofreading, along with providing your welcomed suggested edits. From day one, in spite of your full agenda, you cared about the mission of this project and up until the day that you returned the manuscripts to me—you fulfilled what you said, "I want to do my best work."

To the New Harbor Press publishing assistants. My heart wells up with gratitude toward the thought of each of you being called to do this work for the abused, many years ago; before I even knew of you. As we all know, nothing is a surprise to our Master. The fact that each of you as a team member has been divinely appointed to be a part of this project was orchestrated long ago. I respect your gifts and servanthood toward this ministerial work. I am certain that there are others that unbeknownst to me are or will be a part of the production and delivery of these books and for them I am also grateful. However, I want to take a moment right now to recognize those that I am aware of who have contributed to this work. Thank you Rick Bates-Managing Editor, Pauline Harris-Editor, Steve Nordstrom-Project Manager, Bob Swanson-Typesetting, and Graphic Designer-Natalie Reed. May your service to the abused and helpers of the abused be rewarded a hundredfold!

ACKNOWLEDGMENTS

Thank you to all of my educational, clinical, and spiritual mentors past and present who have selflessly given of your time, wisdom, planted seeds in me, trained and coached me. Your mentoring is an eternal gift which I will treasure and continue to pass on.

My deep appreciation goes to my family of origin, and a tribute to my late parents for their influence in my life. I'm grateful to my immediate family and dear friends who have supported the writing of these books by lovingly standing back, allowing me the flexibility and space, and for praying, so that God's perfect timing would develop the books.

NOTE ON SELECTED TERMINOLOGY

FOR THE PURPOSE OF readability and in an effort to select short universal terms, I have elected to use the words *abuse*, *abuser*, *spouse*, and *victim*. Abuse is used as a term that can involve all forms and levels of victim and family violence: emotional, physical, sexual, economic, and spiritual. This book is not intended to be offensively sexist when the male gender is referred to as the abuser and the female gender is referred to as the victim. My true desire and motive for this book is that it becomes a manual for any person interested in helping those affected by the devastation of family violence.

To maintain a clear and simple discussion throughout the book, I at times refer to the husband or wife as the *spouse*. When referring to the *perpetrator*, I have selected the shorter term, *abuser*, not because I believe that every man who has problems with controlling behaviors is an abuser, but because it is a word that applies to any man who has consistent, ongoing problems with disrespecting, devaluing, and controlling behaviors toward his spouse. When I refer to a spouse, it's not to imply that premarital abuse doesn't exist; in most cases the abuse begins *before* the marriage and goes undetected or ignored until the consummation of the marriage. I have elected to use the term *he* to refer to the abusive spouse. This is not about denigrating men—it's the *mindset* of abusive men that the research addresses, not their manhood. The term *he* is used because the term describes the majority of the research done on relationships in which power and control are misused by men. The research in the June 28, 2013 U.S. Department of Justice, Bureau of Justice Statistics Report documented ninety-five percent of victims of domestic violence are women.

When writing about the woman that is being abused, I use the term *victim,* not because I view that woman as a helpless dupe but because it is a term that applies to any woman suffering from some act(s) of violence that has led her to have severe recurring feelings of intimidation, humiliation, confusion, anxiousness, fear, and/or depression. In selecting women as my victimization sample, I am not doing so to infer that men are not abused. If you know of a man that is in an abusive relationship with his wife, there is information in this book for him as well. Wives that abuse their husbands share the same socialization, background, history, and dynamics as abusive men do. Female abusers use the same tactics, rationalizations, and excuses for their behavior as male abusers. Husbands that are consistently abused by their wives have the same characteristics as wives that are victims of abuse. So read on; you will just have to change the gender language to fit the experience of the abused husband.

In order to incorporate every potential counselor (that may have an opportunity to work with family violence), I have selected the term *professional* or simultaneously the word "*helper*" as opposed to using the title of each mental health practitioner

NOTE ON SELECTED TERMINOLOGY

and clergy member. The word "professional" is not used to infer that laypeople are not capable of ministering or working professionally with victims of abuse. The "professional" or "*helper*" is referred to in the masculine pronoun for the sake of uniformity and word simplicity (applies to both female and male professionals).

The narrative stories that are recounted in this book are all authentic. They are offered as a supplement to the research studies and treatment strategies cited and are intended for both the victim and the helper to recognize the various types of abuse and to encourage both, that it is possible for a victim to heal from the trauma of abuse. They are the victims' personal experiences and perceptions of abuse, as told to this writer. Each story has their given name left out, and the victim (now an *Overcomer*) has selected a name with which to be identified. For the victim's and *overcomer's* protection and privacy, other identifying factors are not disclosed. The abuser's name and all identifying data have been changed. Any similarities to a reader or circumstances of an individual are simply a resemblance as each of these biographies have been tape recorded, reviewed by the subject, and documented for publication with the subject's signed consent. Permission has been obtained from all research study subjects and case scenario examples cited in this book; if any similarities are recognized, it is purely coincidental. The color purple is the official color that is symbolic for family violence awareness; it is used in the book cover, in memory of those victims known and unknown that have been killed by their abusers.

The name "God," His proper names, and pronouns referring to God are capitalized out of reverence to Him. Since capitalization is like italicization, it's a method that suggests "importance" and emphasis; I have elected not to extol satan's name, thus his name is not capitalized. Because God the Father, God the Son, and God the Holy Spirit are One in the same trinity, I am referring to the three of them simultaneously when I'm speaking of our Heavenly Father, since they are each equal as one God (Genesis 1:1-2, 1 John 5:7, John 10:30, Matthew 3:16-17, Matthew 28: 18-19, 2 Corinthians 13:14). The word *Overcomer* is capitalized as a proper noun and given importance because the word represents Jesus; it is also set apart from the other text for emphasis.

All Scriptural quotations are from The Holy Bible, New King James Version. The same Scriptural references may be quoted in parts of this book in order to expand on the verse, use it in a different context, or facilitate comprehension through a different example.

When referring to the victim's *soul,* I am referring to her emotional and moral sense of identity. When speaking of the victim's immaterial being, which is the nerve center for her feelings and sentiments, I speak of her *heart*. I am not using the term soul in a theological form as her immortal part of her being. Conversely, when I refer to her spirit, I am then speaking about her mood or immortal and eternal soul. The Spirit (Holy Spirit) is always capitalized.

The term *mindful* is used to describe the process of becoming aware of one's thinking as related to the mental technique of *mindfulness*, not as in a religious ritual, but as conscious mindful observations of one's thoughts, experiences, and behaviors.

Last, but not least, why the term *Overcomer*? While working with victims of abuse, I have always elected not to use the term "survivor" when referring to any victim that has recovered from abuse. The reason for not using the term "survivor" is that I don't believe in working with victims just to help them exist; I want to encourage them to *stop* living a life of abuse—to permanently conquer and have victory over abuse! Definitions of *survivor* include "to remain alive or in existence, live on." Some synonyms for *survive* are "ride out, weather, and make it through." A victim

NOTE ON SELECTED TERMINOLOGY

doesn't just want to weather and ride out his/her abuse or make it through his/her trauma—he/she wants a fixed line of defense.

The Greek word *Overcomer* literally translated means "victor." The verb (action) forms and noun (person) forms for *overcome* are "to conquer" (conqueror), "to have victory" (victor), and "to defeat" (defeater). The definition of "overcome," and to be an *"Overcomer,"* is more fitting to the desire of every victim of abuse—and ought to be the desire of every society. One cannot say "survivor" while saying "victory." One cannot say "victory" while saying "survivor." One can only say "victory" while saying *"Overcomer."*

> "Bear one another's burdens, and
> so fulfill the law of Christ."
>
> - Galatians 6:2 -

THE PURPOSE OF THESE BOOKS

THIS ENCYCLOPEDIC GUIDEBOOK FOR helpers of abuse was created through the work done with individuals experiencing the dynamics of family abuse. My clinical sources for this book are the victim and the abuser. Both my research and experience with these soldiers, clients, inmates, and patients have consistently indicated the same end results: No matter what class, cultural, ethnic, or racial background they come from, the dynamics of the victim of abuse remain the same; the dynamics for the abuser are consistently the same. There is universality in the characteristics of the hundreds of victims and abusers that my colleagues and I have researched and worked with in the past four decades.

It is my intent to share in this book a body of knowledge on the trauma of abuse. This book articulates research and treatment strategies and provides victim case scenario stories to encourage the helper that there is hope and that positive results are reachable in the treatment of victim abuse. My goal is to encourage lay people, first responders, medical, military, and civilian mental health professionals to receive this message: that victim abuse is preventable and treatable; that the cycle of abuse can be stopped *before* it begins with the next generation. The purpose of this book is trifold.

In the first place, it is to provide a comprehensive resource for those that work with victims of abuse and ultimately to empower women who are involved in an abusive relationship into permanent recovery—through your support—so that victims can be set free from the cycle of abuse and their abuser.

Secondly, this guidebook teaches helpers how to identify an abuser to prevent victims from getting involved in an abusive relationship(s) again.

Thirdly, imbedded in that effort is my goal to empower lay people, families, and our society as a whole with an awareness and understanding of family violence through education on the trauma of abuse, including etiology prevention and intervention.

Will the abuser be pleased that the victim is receiving guidance from you? Absolutely not. However, most victims are not able to leave an abusive relationship without supportive assistance; the majority of victims are unaware or uncertain as to whether their spouses' behavior should be classified as abusive.

By educating yourself on the dynamics of abuse, you can help the victim to clarify the definition of abuse. Even if the victim's spouse's behavior doesn't fit the definition of abuse—if the spouse is consistently controlling and disrespectful—there is still a problem. A victim who has a disrespectful and controlling relationship with her spouse has a problem with abuse.

Controlling spouses fall on a range of behavioral tactics (as discussed in Volume I Part II Abuser Characteristics) from exhibiting only *some* tactics to exhibiting *most* of them. All of the recurring thoughts and feelings that a victim experiences may

THE PURPOSE OF THESE BOOKS

still have an unhealthy effect. Abuse ranges from *mild* to *severe*; nevertheless, all abuse has the same impact on the victim (See Volume I Part III, Victim Characteristics).

It is highly recommended that all helpers of abuse victims, before engaging in a supportive relationship with a victim, become well-informed about the characteristics of victims, abusers, reconciliation advisors, and those that are recovered from abuse—*Overcomers.*

It is not recommended that readers skim read Volume I, II, or III, as this can lead to a misinterpretation of the contents and a misunderstanding of treatment modalities and the overall message.

However, readers will understand that since Volume I, II, and III were designed as encyclopedic guidebooks, they may refer back to necessary sections as they have time during the course of treatment with specific victim cases.

The strategic way for the victim to step out of her abusive relationship is for you to give her permission to take charge of her person. Encourage her to focus on reclaiming her pre-abused self, and if children are involved to claim her children's well-being as well. Overcoming abuse is a safety-risk journey for the victim. It is an evolving process, a process that through your supportive, well-grounded treatment strategies can heal and resolve the abuse.

Through your assistance, the victim will no longer carry the burden of an abusive relationship alone. Your guidance and assistance can lead her to freedom from abuse!

Some victims feel guilty for confiding in someone or are fearful of being betrayed and that the abuser will find out if confidentiality is broken. They may feel scared about speaking negatively to anyone about their spouse, or they may be ashamed of their spouse's abusive behavior.

Victims sometimes worry that the person whom they tell will judge them for continuing to tolerate this abuse. A lot of victims fear that they will not be believed because, after all, their spouse is such a hard-working family man, and in the eyes of the church, employer, or his community, he's an upstanding citizen.

Regardless, in order to heal, be set free from the trauma of abuse, and to obtain peace of mind, surrendering her abusive relationship and seeking support is absolutely necessary. Trust and fear are foundational feelings to a victim who attempts to break her silence and her cycle of abuse.

Having you as her trustworthy, knowledgeable support system is a *vital* part of problem-solving her abuse. Establishing your consistent support will expedite her healing process in the overcoming of her abuse.

This book is dedicated to lay persons and professional counselors who are interested in supporting the victim in her decision to overcome her abuse.

A recovering victim or *Overcomer* is invited to read Volume III after she finishes Volume I and II, and a helper of victims of abuse is encouraged to read Volume I and II.

There are some helpers who have not had the opportunity to receive as much information about the trauma of abuse as they would like to. Volume I, II, and III were written with the intent of educating the victim, society, *and* helpers of the abused.

Some sections will contain small excerpts from Volume I and II so that the helper can obtain significant information which the victim has received in Volume I and II as a part of her recovery process.

Furthermore, an excerpt may be used to maintain fluency and connection between the three volumes or to cover a very important part of working with victims, such as the development of a Safety Escape Plan.

THE PURPOSE OF THESE BOOKS

Volume III was specifically developed for all individuals to learn how to best help the victim. Volume III is offered for the purpose of increasing abuse awareness, education, and the number of persons in the population who are willing to stand in the gap, step out and step-up to stop, and overcome abuse in our society.

> **"Let each of you look out not only for his own interests, but also for the interests of others."**
>
> **- Philippians 2:4 -**

PART I

AMERICA'S HISTORY OF ABUSE

Women as Men's Property

IT ALWAYS HELPS TO know the origin of something in order to fully comprehend *how* it has come to be an accepted part of our lives. You see, society once sanctioned violence against women. Abuse, as you are experiencing it now in our society has been a part of our history since Roman times. When the Romans designed the family as a legal structure (to ensure the transmission of property to the male heirs), they of course didn't have DNA paternity testing; only a woman could ever know for sure who a child's father was. Men at that time controlled women as progenitors in order to pass on their property to their rightful descendants. However, marital laws and the punishment of wives were not always about transfer of property, as Dobash and Dobash wrote: "The reason was not so much about thwarted love but loss of control and damage to a possession. Women were the chattels of their husbands, and as pieces of property it was important that they remain under the control of, and in the possession of, their owner."[1]

O'Faolain and Martines wrote: "Control of wives was of the utmost importance to the Romans, and it was expected that this task be carried out by the husband in the privacy of his own home rather than become a public matter. Accordingly, lawmakers and public officials preferred not to interfere in domestic affairs. Roman husbands had the legal right to chastise, divorce or kill their wives for engaging in behavior that they engaged in themselves daily ... If she were caught attending public games without his permission, or walking outdoors with her face uncovered, she could be beaten."[2] The attitude about a woman's role being inferior and for the purpose of subjugation was not confined to the Roman era. This same male orientation on how women were to be treated was equilateral between the Western culture and across the world continents. In the early nineteenth century, both Western and American courts acknowledged that it was a husband's right to beat his wife with a stick as long as it was "no thicker than his thumb."

In 1848, slavery was still legal in most of the U.S. and regardless of color, the social standing of *all* women was subordinate to men. "Women—regardless of color—could not own property or keep their wages if they were married; women could not draft a will; women were barred from filing lawsuits in court, including suits seeking custody of their children; women could not attend college; and husbands were widely viewed as having unquestioned authority over their wives and children."[3] It was during this period of time that approximately three hundred women wagon-trailed from every part of the U.S. to upstate New York and gathered at the Wesleyan Chapel in the town of Seneca Falls to challenge their second-class citizenship.

AMERICA'S HISTORY OF ABUSE

These women were led by Elizabeth Cady Stanton, who requested that women's basic rights and opportunities be expanded, including the right to vote. Many that attended the conference were *shocked* by these ideas. Elizabeth Stanton's husband rode out of town in protest; a lot of folks thought such a proposal seemed "absurd and outrageous!" And so it is, that, centuries back it was considered legal for husbands to beat or kill their spouses in exchange for providing for them; they were allowed to control their wives' behavior in the "privacy of their own home." Some laws have been modified or changed since the Seneca Falls town convention, and many of Elizabeth Stanton's proposals are now accepted as constitutional fairness and rights. But, due to this sociological historical origin in Western and U.S. society, some men have still been raised to view women with an attitude of a lower scale of social standing. Today, many men continue to dominate and control women abusively, for our society has had a history of being tolerant of the nature of this behavior. The early history of women has left its mark with the mental conditioning that has developed throughout the centuries; that is what contaminates the attitudes toward women up until the current times.

Sin as the Origin of Abuse
As for the Christian historical origin of today's abusive relationships between men and women, that origin can be explained and summed up in one word—sin. Most of us have read or heard of the first humans that God created, Adam and Eve (Genesis 1-2). We are *all* historical descendants of Adam and Eve. They were innocent of willful evildoing until the serpent (satan) tempted them into willful guilty disobedience of God (Genesis 3, Revelation 12:9). The serpent not only tempted Eve by talking her into disobeying God, but Adam stood by and did not make *any* attempt to protect Eve from the serpent or talk her out of

disobeying (engaging in sin). This willful disobedience (sin) is usually referred to as the fall of all humankind. This fall (sin) caused us to be born into sin which corrupted our human nature and our society. Numerous acts of violence are recorded in the Bible after the fall of mankind. The initial conflict generated from abusive rage is recorded as Cain killing his brother Abel (Genesis 4:6-8). All of these acts of violence are sin.

In his book *Whatever Became of SIN?* Dr. Karl Menninger, renowned psychiatrist and author, wrote:

> "The very word 'sin,' which seems to have disappeared, was a proud word. It was once a strong word, an ominous and serious word. It described a central point in every civilized human being's life plan and lifestyle. But the word went away. It has almost disappeared—the word, along with the notion. Why? Doesn't anyone sin anymore? Doesn't anyone believe in sin?"[4]

Dr. Menninger documented and recognized the avoidance of the word sin as a disappearing act by the American culture; he attested that in place of America's historic concept of sin, our society now speaks of "crime" and "symptoms." Dr. Menninger's alarm to Americans is that when we look at sin as crime or symptoms, we are missing the mark on morality—right and wrong behavior. God has moral laws—they're called commandments. Crime is a moral problem. Crime is a sin, such as it was with Cain when he murdered his brother Abel. This was not just a problem between Cain and Abel; it also involved God because sin (crime) is committed between a person and God.

Dr. Menninger's book is well-taken. If you turn sin into crime, this means that God has been taken out of the truth from what really happened—sin. This is what America has done with the abuser's symptoms and crime: it has disacknowledged sin. In his book, he notes that when "sin" is substituted for the word "symptoms," it is now defined as a condition that's on the exterior of the individual (it's due to his circumstances, environment) outside of his control. America has found a way to lose sight of the act of sin; it has decided that sin is not an act from within and should be blamed on the outside of the person's being. It appears that, when pertaining to the crime (sin) of abuse, America has four choices. It can continue to deny it; it can continue allowing it to increase; it can be worked out by each person on their own (which is not possible); *or* America can admit to sin (crime). With America's disappearing act on *"sin,"* that word has become meaningless in society. This is why our culture accepts victim abuse and family violence as a norm; America has turned away from the law of God. Sin cannot be a part of our culture without involving God's law and vice versa. Where families stand in their boundaries and moral codes, our culture will stand. If our family boundaries for abuse fall short and disintegrate, the culture will fall short too.

In contemporary society, the abuser's behaviors are defined as *domestic violence*; not as a crime, let alone as sin. Yes, some states in the U.S. consider domestic violence an illegal act, but not all of the aspects of domestic violence are defined as abuse (see Volume I types of abuse Part I) or considered criminal in the legal system. For example, victims who allege severe, immoral, emotional abuse by the abuser toward them and their children are ignored when they request protective orders, and the abuser continues to be allowed interactions with the victim and the children. The disavowal of the abuser's crime in a society that has almost made God and sin disappear makes for a culture of the acceptance of victim abuse. Many have asked the questions: "What is wrong with the American traditional (moral) family?" "Why is the traditional American family disintegrating?" The answer is self-explanatory. What is wrong with the traditional American family is a result of each one of us in society. We've gone astray—and the culture of America allows it, encourages it, and enables it.

Religion and Women as Property
One can evaluate and re-evaluate many of the factors as to how women became viewed as men's property and worthy of being disrespected and mistreated, and one can reach many speculations and conclusions. But there's one factor that doesn't hold; *that is*, the one that has been alleged about religion playing a role in the subjugation of women as property. Some religious denominations may engage in dehumanizing women into property and subjecting them to abuse, but not all religions view women as property. It is just *some* religious individuals that play a role in such condescension. Yes, it is true that some religious leaders of various denominations support the view that women are less than adequate and basically man's property. For instance, Saint Thomas Aquinas, a renowned theologian and philosopher wrote, "For father and mother are loved as principles of our natural origin. Now the father is principle in a more excellent way than the mother, because he is the active principle, while the mother is a passive and material principle. Consequently, strictly speaking, the father is to be loved more."[5]

Saint Augustine, a Roman era Christian theologian, whose sermons and written work continue to influence Western Christianity said, "but separately, as helpmate, the woman herself alone is not the image of God; whereas the man alone is the image of God."

Then there was Martin Luther, known for his role as a Protestant Reformation leader; he is quoted saying, "Men have broad shoulders and narrow hips and accordingly they possess intelligence. Women have narrow shoulders and broad hips.

Women ought to stay at home; the way they were created indicates this, for they have broad hips and a fundamental to sit upon, keep house and bear and raise children."[6]

Table Talk also known as the Weimarer Ausgabe writings on Luther (or "TR"), clearly documents *Luther's* condescending words and opinions about woman's intelligence, purpose for her body, her worth and her appropriate role in relation to men. "There is no dress that suits a woman or maiden so badly as wanting to be clever" (WA, TR II, no. 1555, p. 130). Martin Luther laughed at his wife, who wanted to be clever, and said, "God created man with a broad chest, not broad hips, so that in that part of him he can be wise; but that part out of which filth comes is small. In a woman this is reversed. That is why she has much filth and little wisdom" (WA, TR II, no. 1975, p. 285). "When women speak well, it is not praiseworthy. It befits them to stammer and not be able to speak well; that adorns them much better" (WA, TR IV, no. 4081, pp. 121-122). Luther filtered down his ideas and views of womankind; he was and continues to be held by many in high reverence.

It is important to remember that these are St. Thomas Aquinas's beliefs, St. Augustine's and Martin Luther's opinion of woman. *It is not the belief or opinion of their religion.* Men of various religions can have deep-set ideas on how they view women, but it is *not* necessarily the shared representative opinion of religion. Although Aquinas, Augustine and Luther wrote many worthy insights, their theology on women was not aligned with our Creator's view of women. Some individuals totally miss *God's divine viewpoint* on His Creation—woman. Martin Luther for instance, although a respected renowned theologian, very obviously *overlooked* the part of God's instructions on how women are to be treated.

God actually shows His mercy and protection of women throughout the Bible. One example is found in Numbers 5:11-31 when He established a judicial procedure for women, when they were falsely accused of infidelity by their jealous husbands. God set in place for women not to be beaten or killed by their suspicious husbands; instead they were able to have "a right to a fair trial" before an impartial judge. This justice and triumphalism for innocent women in biblical times assures women victims today of the power and victory in knowing God and the existence of His love for womankind.

It does not matter how many churches and religious leaders have been known to practice bringing women under control in the name of biblical *submission*. Anyone who has ever attended an evangelical church and heard their sermons or has read the Bible knows that Jesus' teachings on submission were not about controlling women—that is false teaching. It is loud and clear through the Bible; Jesus warned us all that there would be false prophets on His teachings: "For false prophets will rise and show signs and wonders to deceive, if possible, even the elect" (Mark 13:22). Regarding the false and true teaching of God's love and plan for mankind (including women) Jesus said: "Beware of false prophets, who come to you in sheep's clothing, but inwardly they are ravenous wolves" (Matthew 7:15).

The truth is that nowhere in the Bible does it state that God's view of woman is that she is material principle (man's property); or that man is the one that possesses intelligence; or that the father is to be loved more; or that God views man independently more valuable than woman. On the contrary: "Honor your father and your mother" (Exodus 20:12). 1 Corinthians 11:11-12 states, "Nevertheless, neither is man independent of woman, nor woman independent of man, in the Lord. For as woman came from man, even so man also comes through woman; but all things are from God." Even as a couple, God's Word states that as husband and wife, they are equally together heirs of His grace! (1 Peter 3:7).

Those who profess that religion is to blame for the way society views and treats women are trampling over God Who in fact upholds womankind. Jesus Himself set the pace for mankind and *how* women are to be viewed and treated. Jesus *affirmed women* and *set them free*. It was to a woman that Jesus gave the privilege as being the first to see Him after His resurrection. If there was not an equal opportunity for women with God, then clearly He could have elected a man to be the first eyewitness to His rising from the dead. Jesus never spoke of assigned class roles for women. He *respected* the women He encountered and viewed them as individuals in their own right. Jesus was *kind* and *compassionate* toward women. In both miracles that He performed whereby He raised persons from the dead, it was to restore loved ones *to women* (the widow that got her only son back, and Mary and Martha who got their beloved brother, Lazarus, back) (Luke 7:11-17, John 11:1-44).

Neither by His words nor by His actions did Jesus ever instruct for women to be disparaged. Jesus' interactions with women in the Bible demonstrated His treatment of them with respect, honoring their dignity, and accepting their self-evidence. The Bible's accounts on women are simply that God looked upon them as human beings—just like the men. God called women like Miriam, Rahab, Lois, Esther, Abigail, Eunice, Deborah, Dorcas, Naomi, Ruth, Mary, Elizabeth, Sarah, Hannah, Junia, and others into prominent leadership roles right along with the men. Jesus' meeting with and attitude toward the Samaritan woman at the well (John 4) was no different back then than it is today. In His heart, woman is forgiven, like all of His children—she's free and favored (certainly, not anyone's property). Jesus role-modeled how women are to be treated: God set a standard for us to follow; we are responsible for passing that standard to others.

There is no difference today as to how Jesus viewed women in biblical times. When God created man and woman, He said it was "very good." The Bible remains the same as God: the same yesterday, today, and forevermore. God's principles remain the same and are applicable today. God's view of women will always be the same. Regardless of God (Father, Son, and Holy Spirit) treating women *without* discrimination and freeing them from condemnation, the same cannot be said of society during biblical times or society in the twenty-first century. It is people in a society who *construct* positive or negative characteristics that are assigned to a gender role. Stratification of women comes from the world—not God. There is no special gender-specific requirement for God to *love* us and view us as worthy of respect— it is available to *any human being* who has *faith* in Him (Matthew 15:28).

Historical View of Women Must Change

Has there been *significant* change historically regarding how men view and treat or mistreat women? I can only attest to what I have personally observed, read, researched, or worked with. I grew up in New York City, and I had the privilege of going through the civil rights movement. I can say that I witnessed *some* progress in the 1970s when there was a breakthrough, and the media captured and showed footage of women speaking out about crimes against women and bringing public awareness. Currently, the Federal Bureau of Investigation reports that every fifteen seconds a woman is beaten by her abuser. According to statistics, by November 30, 2012 there were 6,614 U.S. troops killed in Afghanistan and Iraq. The number of women killed in the U.S. by their abuser, in the same time period was 11,766. In 2013 the Department of Justice recorded ninety-two percent of all domestic violence incidents, crimes, as committed by men against women.

I believe the question of *"has there been any historical change in the way women are viewed and treated,"* is best answered through seeking conclusions from hypothetical questions and observations such as: Has there been any change in how *involved* contemporary society, the media, social media, first responders, the police, and the judicial system are in protecting women before and after they become victims of mistreatment and family violence? *Who* is allowing pornography, casinos, human trafficking, and prostitution (thus encouraging undervalued displays of and violence against women and sexualizing them)? Are boys being trained to become abusive, aggressive men? Are the family unit, educational system, government, economy, and mass media, promoting violence against women? How did we become a society that tolerates abuse and allows it to exist? Are there investors, lawmakers, and policy makers that run our society's tolerance for abuse? Who are the moneygrubbers and profit makers in our society that allow abuse to prevail? Does religion play a role in *why* women stay in abusive relationships? Are there more men or women victims of abuse in our society?

In answering the aforementioned questions, we are more able to determine how women are being viewed in contemporary society. The answers to those questions reveal *many* examples which indicate that, historically, not much has changed. If *anything* has changed, it has been *gradual* and *is still* in serious need of repair. Have you ever noticed the colorful mosaics of barely draped women in museums or castles (ceilings, walls, or floors) whether overseas, or in the U.S.? These disrobed or nude images of women have left the ceilings, walls, and floors and made their way pioneered into avant-garde displays of women in pornographic magazines and audio-visuals; even into our family rooms through recurring provocative advertisements.

Since ancient history and up to the present, why do women have to be nude in order to be displayed in some galleries and museums of art? Even today, you can accidently walk into a restaurant and have some scantily clad female food server greet you and offer for her underdressed cohorts to wait on you at your table, whereas generally a barely-dressed male food server will not appear to serve you. Where are the honorable mentions, respect, and value for women in the message of these sorts of food servers? This discussion is not to infer that women are *never* to be looked at and admired—there's a difference between perverted, lustful gawking and *pure* admiration of God's creation.

This discussion is about the way God intended for His creation—woman—to be looked at and treated: He created her in His Image; she is to be looked at and treated with respect. 1 Peter 3:7 instructs a husband to dwell with his wife with understanding and to give her honor. God is clear about His regard for and purpose for woman. The definition of the word *respect* includes the condition of being esteemed or honored *to be held in respect*. Both men and women in today's society are receiving the message that women were created for man's purposes. Nowhere in God's Word does it instruct men to use women as pieces of property for their pleasure, purpose, or services, or to use, misuse, and abuse them, and to seek another piece of property when they tire of their first piece of property.

Historically there have been and currently are strip clubs, "gentlemen's" clubs, spas, and massage parlors where females work to sexually entertain males. Exploiting women's bodies in public is offered by our society as a form of sexual recreation for men, from topless bars, to thong swimsuits and wet tee-shirt contests, to pole dancing, providing sexual favors in casinos and clubs, sex date call girls or via phone sex or the internet. There have been and continue to be fashion trends that focus on showing women's skin and sexual parts. Currently there are naked evening and bridal gowns, naked swimsuits, and naked underwear. Why do women have to wear apparel that makes them appear naked? Tall, beautiful females with what men consider voluptuous bodies are hired to pin pointedly stand smiling at the camera behind sports men being interviewed; in toto to advertise with sex appeal.

There is nothing wrong with fashion or product advertising, but why do women have to be vulgarized and degraded in the process of working to market to consumers? Even family daytime or evening game shows have hostesses or game prop women dressed in push up bosom plunging dresses. If it was just one female exhibiting her sexual parts one could conclude, well she just elected to dress sexy today; but why are so many of them barely covered up on national TV? What's equally disturbing is not only that those women have been victimized into accepting this requested entitlement and expectation from men—but that women comply and engage in disrobing themselves in magazines and other forms of media for men's' pleasure and hobby. Women submit themselves daily to be reduced to the level of being publicly seduced as sex objects because society has encouraged and assigned them this role. Does our culture sincerely believe that women will gain *respect* by disrobing and undressing them publicly? *Whose* purposes do undressed, sexually-provocative women serve in our society?

As a society—as the culture of America—we must ask ourselves what is our value for women? What is our *purpose* for women? This query goes beyond addressing the problem of abuse of women and marital abuse. It's also about *the family*. What is our *value* for the family? Is the family just another institution in our society? Is the marital and family institution worth restoring? Are we too busy developing technology that we have no time for the family institution? Is the marital and family institution an antiquated conduit for a set of traditional values (the upholding of the family) that are no longer applicable in the world of the internet, cellphones, tablets, laptops, social media, and drones? What if America would use all of their modern technology to *uphold* and *respect* women and children?

What if America would stop provocatively disrobing women and prohibit violence against women and children on national television and other sources of media?

Marital and any type of abuse is an injustice. This kind of injustice is a symptom of a culture that devalues women and children. How our culture in America responds to the value for womankind and the family will determine whether marital and family abuse can be overcome in our nation. *Respect* and *value* for womankind is vital for a functional family system—for a healthy society. Where are we as a country regarding the freedom and liberty of women and children in *not* allowing their oppression? The only answer that would resolve the problem of how women and the family are viewed is to state with clarity and courage that we are a nation that will *not* tolerate the abuse of women and children!

We *must* respond with conviction that we believe in the protection of women and the family. We *must* enforce that we are energetic and not apologetic regarding the choice to value women and children. We are to become history makers and world changers in stopping marital and family abuse. Our nation's challenge and homework is to remove the apathetic, laid back attitude that only maintains the complacency toward abuse in our households. We must snap out of the indifferent attitude toward abuse and place it in the public limelight by moving the fight against family violence into the mainstream of our culture.

What does America want to be known for now and in the future generations? This question is both a clarion call to victims of abuse and their nation. One can state, "Well, I'm just that way." Well, don't be that way! America can change its culture of abuse and once again lay claim to the stance that we are to protect women and children, not just during times of war, but *at all times*. Why? Because today's negligent outlook on women and children regarding abuse is tomorrow's captivity of the family! Let us offer the culture of our society an alternative to the pathetic disregard that only brings *despair* to the family and its future generations. Let's become change agents in the culture of abuse. We must adhere to the precept: "Future steps have no value until they become the current step that is taken." Let us proactively work on a solution—to *overcome abuse*.

Historically, blaming the victim and keeping the outrage of marital abuse from the public's realm has served not to acknowledge the outcry of the victim. Mankind does not want to hear a horror story; at the cinema yes, but not in real life. They don't want to hear about a wife being held emotionally or forcefully hostage. Have you ever noticed that at the conclusion of a newscast there's an effort to include a quick upbeat story to end the bad news on a lighter note? Bad news is never invited. Like with the newscasters and human viewers, society doesn't want to hear about the horrific things that happen in a victim's home (whether in a secular or Christian household).

The information about the atrocities that have occurred in *relationship abuse* has crossed society historically, but unlike other news and data, it is not documented and recorded as factual. This is because our humanity has the option of flight, fight, or freeze when confronted with the horror of a tragedy (see Part II for more on Cannon's theory of "Flight, Fight, and Freeze"). Frankly, our society has taken the *flight* and *freeze* approach to marital abuse. Denial and the emotional paralysis surrounding this phenomenon have allowed relationship abuse to be an underground chronicled archive that have limited the public awareness of the enormity of abuse cases that go unheard, are given short sentencing or are unprosecuted.

The historical denial and suppression of the large scale of marital abuse that occurs daily across society (without intervention) has delayed the process of the treatment and the healing of family violence. Society contributes to the ongoing spousal abuse by ignoring this type of abuse that infests our nation. This is not to allege that society is to blame as the sole cause of marital abuse; there is no sole cause for the longstanding problem of marital abuse—only well-founded correlations, predisposing evidence, dysfunctional families, empowered abusers, abuse moneymakers, detached attitudes toward family violence, and silence on the subject.

Marital abuse is *real* nevertheless. For centuries there has been a disclaimer on this fact. It's time to make new history in the centuries to come; it's time to stop claiming that the abuser is an impeccable citizen and that the victim is just a damsel in distress! Seeing the victim in this way influences and impedes the direction taken to study and treat marital abuse as a trauma and a crime. In order for the historical disacknowledging of this real social problem to stop, more individuals in our society have to be informed about the *abuser profile* and *victim dynamics* and then actually take action to step up and speak out against the criminal act of abuse. There is power in numbers. When America agrees that it will not be defeated by the abuser, both the victim and society can take a quantum leap toward overcoming the trauma of abuse.

The characteristics of an abuser not only affect each victim; the tragedy of it all is how these characteristics infect our society. In 2013, the Domestic Violence Abuse statistical report from the Department of Justice noted that a child's exposure to the father abusing the mother is the strongest risk factor for transmitting violent behavior from one generation to the next. About sixty-five percent of those abusers that abuse the mother also physically and/or sexually abuse their children. Family violence costs the nation from five to ten billion dollars annually in medical expenses, police and court costs, shelters, foster care, sick leave, absenteeism, and non-productivity. The U.S. health care cost of domestic violence, alone, is 5.8 billion dollars. Up to fifty-percent percent of homeless women and children in the U.S. are fleeing domestic violence.

When it comes to family violence, there is no need for the public to remain uninformed about the private crimes being committed daily by those abusers in the U.S. who rule their spouses as socialist nations do. The disavowal of this social problem by society will only increase the problem and allow it to continue throughout the generations unresolved. Victim abuse, trauma, and death by abuse *cannot* be resolved in the U.S. without societal support of the victim, abuser penalty, and society's accountability (sustained with advocacy against victim and family violence). The problem of family violence in our society has become an acceptable norm because when unusual behaviors are seen repeatedly, they become normal to society.

A society that does not provide advocacy for the victim only enables her victimization and contributes to the family violence and death statistics. Many take the way out by stating that this is not their problem as it's not personally affecting them at the time. Nevertheless, the real truth is that *it is* our society's *entire* problem. The abusers and victims come from every social background in existence. They come representing none or all of the political parties. Needless to say, this has never been about select political parties, so *any* political party can advocate for laws against victim and family violence. This is about men bullying and beating up women and children; this is about a social issue in our society. It is going to take *all* political parties and those that have no party preference to join forces to work on resolving the thinking about marital and family violence, with a united action to change society's mind-set into a *no tolerance* for victim violence.

Victim abuse and family violence is as devastating and useless to humanity and society as military friendly fire is. It's a disgraceful loss of life. If family violence is to be stopped, it has to become a mission for America's defense of the family. We together as a nation can become the family safety net. If family violence is put to a halt, many other societal problems can be resolved simultaneously. The breakdown of the family through violence creates social problems such as: mental and physical illnesses, addictions, unemployment, poverty, homelessness, deviance, criminology, and large governmental economic expenses. It is not all about fixing the symptoms of abuse but also about working on the causes and consequences of family abuse.

America's commitment to protect the family system has to be reborn for family violence to stop. Justice for the victim of abuse in our society has yet to be pioneered. This is because most of our culture is unaware or under-aware of the dynamics of abuse for the victim and her family. Centuries ago, the courts acknowledged the husband's right to beat his wife. What if judges across our nation today would acknowledge and rule that *any type* of abuse is a crime? What if domestic violence became a crime in the U.S. just like it is in the military? Justice in family abuse only becomes an unobtainable ideal when our culture and the judicial system do not work together and instead work against the victims of abuse.

Abolishing family abuse is a collective effort; we must have a social conscience about it. Altruism is not new to America, but it can stand to be refreshed and renewed. One way to change contemporary society's thinking about the victim, the abuser, marital abuse, and the trauma of abuse is by changing society's heart to a heart of compassion for the woman and child as victims—instead of perpetuating the problem. We've got to jump-start our nation's heart for the family and keep recharging it with a spirit of compassion for those victims of the trauma of abuse, which will become our next generation. Change the heart of a people about respect for womankind and you can change their perspective and attitude about overcoming family abuse!

AMERICA'S HISTORY OF ABUSE

Respect for womankind is vital for a functional family—for a healthy society. If we join together on disallowing the crime of *any type of abuse* toward women and children, our nation can become an inviolable sanctuary for the family. As century follows century and victims of the crime of abuse are ignored, the need for the recognition of the existence of the dynamics of abuse trauma and action against this crime becomes greater and greater.

Changing society's perspective on the trauma of abuse to viewing it as a crime that needs to be confronted, treated, and brought to justice is *not* about women's liberation and a feminist agenda; it's a "matter of life and death" movement to restore and heal human victims' lives. It's also a revolutionary revival for the family system—so that the mission to put a stop to family violence can be fulfilled. Society needs a new mission statement for the women and children of America. We are commissioned to love one another. The same compassion of a missionary around the globe can become a standard national compassionate mission in our American society—to disallow the criminal activity of any type of abuse against women and children.

> "He who calls you *is* faithful,
> who also will do *it*."
>
> - 1 Thessalonians 5:24 -

SUZANNE'S STORY

I MET SAM IN fourth grade—at church. We grew up in the South. We both accepted salvation as children and attended activities together all the way up to youth group. Our parents knew one another, and were friends. We began to date our junior year in high school; my parents were fond of Sam. I had gone directly from high school to secretarial school (it was the "bride" thing to do). My parents never pushed me to go to college because Dad was an executive and Mom had not gone to school (but it worked out just fine for her); it was just the culture at the time. We were barely twenty when Sam and I decided to marry—it was a huge wedding! We continued being active in church. Sam even rededicated his life to Christ when he got older; he became a deacon. We have two children from this marriage, a daughter and son. I became a stay-at-home mom for six and a half years. After that, I worked part-time outside of the home. Between Sam's employer and my salary, we put Sam through college; he has a bachelor's degree.

As I reflect back on the times *when we were dating,* I can now see that he had a *rage* issue. Sam seemed to have a very short temper, but only ten percent of the time; the rest of the time he was a *very nice* guy! I thought I could love him out of that (I was a teenager); I thought I could do anything! My thinking was that I could fix that part, but as time passed that part got bigger and bigger, and the nice guy got smaller and smaller. Sam's temper became very unpredictable; his anger was very hostile and abusive in the way that he talked to me. Sam had a displeased nature about him; he would let it be known that *whatever* I did (even things that I knew would be pleasing to him) they were *not good enough*. Sam would speak to me in demeaning ways and undermine anything that I did; he would acknowledge something I did but would follow it up with, "that's fine but you *didn't* do this..." Once, I even wrote up all the things that I was doing, then wrote up all that he told me that I wasn't doing and I presented it to him to show him how I was making things happen; I said, here it is on paper. I did that just to keep my sanity!

Soon after that, I went to my doctor and I was telling him about the stress in my life. I told my doctor that it was "this or the other" that was causing my husband to be the way that he was. My doctor looked at me and asked, "Is he *mean*?" It was the *best* question, because I sat there for a minute and finally responded with, "oh yeah, he is *mean*!" I pondered some more and knew that being mean is a choice. It was *then* that I started listening to and looking at Sam's ways with me, and decided mentally at each incident, "that was mean!" My doctor's question about meanness started helping me to see the meanness in Sam. Sam's escalated nature got even worse after our second child was born; it seemed that the more attention that the children needed, the more out-of-control his temper got. Sam was more explosive now and infuriated by the time that was being devoted to our children; and part of it appeared to be connected to more responsibility being required of him. But it also became clear that he had experienced a really weird childhood. Sam disclosed that there were things that our children got that he never experienced, such as loving protection, and he appeared to be jealous of our kids.

Sam said that his mother's father had been abusive toward her, so when she married Sam's dad she had decided that she was not going to allow any abuse, and she overprotected herself by constantly verbally annihilating Sam's dad. *She* was caustic and her husband was *passive,* and he didn't think of comebacks as fast as she did. Sam had three brothers; they watched their mother verbally take their dad down! They decided they were *never* going to allow any woman to do that to them. In Sam's family the role choices in marriage were either be a bully or a victim. Sam's brothers ended up being abusive toward their wives. It was obvious that while I was married to Sam, my three sisters-in-law were also being abused. One day I was visiting with my sisters-in-law about our husbands' abuse, and one of them piped in that her husband said that she was, "just imagining it." My other sisters-in-law and I turned to her in a chorus and said, "Mine says that to me all the time!" After I heard that, I realized that I *myself* was beginning to think that *I was* imagining things. It makes you crazy—it's craze-making! You begin to doubt your own self and ask, "Am I being oversensitive?" When the three of us talked and put that together, we just looked at each other and knew it was for real. There are currently six former missuses in Sam's family; someday I guess we'll have a convention in heaven!

Now, in my family we had some male domination going on. My dad was a type-A personality, very driven, and my mom—who knows what type she was?! Dad always said he thought mom was "cute"—so it worked! My dad could be gruff with my mom; he was *never* a bully and certainly not abusive toward her. But dad would talk down to mom at times and she would tolerate it more than she should have; she was doing it out of respect for him, she wrapped it in that submissive wives' cure. She and

I both know *now* that that's a bunch of malarkey. However, my parents grew in their relationship. As they grew spiritually and learned more, they gained mutual respect for one another—their marriage was transformed as they went along. By the time I got to high school, the entire male domination thing was not happening near as much, and by the time dad retired, it wasn't happening anymore! They were married fifty-four years until dad passed away.

Sam and I remained married for sixteen years; I was the one to request the divorce. Sam had told me at this point that he hated my guts and he basically never came off of that position, but I had hung in there because I didn't believe that I had a biblical reason to divorce him. For many years I wanted to end the relationship; it was a *miserable* place to be, but I was there because I told God that I would be there in my vow to Him and my kids. One day God provided a biblical reason for my divorce in the form of an email; it contained *everything* anyone would ever need to request a divorce from their spouse. I accidently opened up an email thinking it was from my sister, sending me photos of her family. Instead, it was a woman sending naked pictures of her to my husband! The email discussed things they had done and plans for what they were going to do, and he had replied positively. At the time I had three people praying with me for a resolution because living with my husband the way things were wasn't working; I didn't feel any freedom as an individual. Finding the email was like the key to a cage. Even after finding the email I prayed for a month; more than I've ever prayed for anything. I was praying that God would be clear. I listened and one day I heard His voice ask, "What are you going to do about the email?" At that point it became clear that I was free!

I wasn't free of the *sadness*, and the attack that divorce brings into the self, our children, people, other marriages, and the church. But, from that point forward, I have *never* had a second thought and I always wondered if I would. My father was an elder in the church; I knew my decision would have an impact on our entire congregation. I was tied to the phone over the next four months! I have no regrets about the divorce; all of the elements of adultery were there, he had been emotionally abusive toward me and verbally harsh with the kids, he had backed our young son up to the wall, and he had been on drugs. At times, when he would get so angry, I would leave the house with the kids *crying* and just drove around because I didn't know if he would hurt the kids. I had gone to my dad for guidance and his response had been that you have to have a biblical reason for divorce—and my heart was always hung up on that! Since then, I've learned through a divorce care group, that you have to be able to say before God, "I did *everything* that I needed to do and it didn't work." If I had known what I know now about abuse, I would have probably felt free to leave sooner and would have reached that spiritual peace. I was the first to divorce in my family of origin—in both sides of my parent's family—this is just *not* something that we did; other people do that!

Deciding on the divorce was an extremely difficult financial place to be. Sam had lost his job several times because he was a jerk and got fired! But even then, he was still a big spender and wanted me to be a stay-at-home mom. Our children were now nine and seven. Sam refused to move out when I asked him for the divorce and to please leave. I had to leave to go to my parents', with the only amount of money left in our savings account—forty-five dollars. When I told my parents that I was getting a divorce, my dad asked how much money I had. When I said forty-five dollars, my dad's response was that they had seen this coming *for a long time* and they had already talked about it; they offered to buy a larger home so that the kids and I could move in with them. They had recently built their dream retirement home but put it up on the market for us. This was a precious gift—my kids and I lived with them for five years. That was a safe haven for the kids to grow up in, a great neighborhood with lots of kids, and my parents were there for them when I was working and couldn't be home.

Sam attempted to harass me after the divorce, several times, but he knew better than to come near me because he knew my father had his bluff! Also, Sam had a positive relationship with my dad (which had been going on since childhood). Because of my father, Sam didn't do a lot of things that I believe he would have done otherwise.

I didn't keep Sam away from the kids because I always thought that the kids needed a dad in their lives, even if their dad was a little crazy. At least not in my "Bible church nuclear family" background type of thinking, I never thought that the kids didn't need their dad. I thought it was important for the kids to know their dad. One day Sam showed up to tell us that he had decided to move out of state; the kids were feeling *completely abandoned*! While my parents and I were in the front yard *dancing*.

Sam just up and went away. I believe that was very much a God thing to remove him; because he was telling our son things like, "Mom got a divorce because of all of the women calling the house." My response was, "What, there were women calling our house?" Sam was playing head games with our son, so much so that by age eleven, our son ended up in residential care for suicidal ideation. I found out from our son, in a family therapy session, that Sam had been asking him to hit and attack me; so that the police would come and give *Sam* custody. My son said that he was torn because he was trying to please his dad, but he couldn't bring himself to attack me. My son said that he knew it was wrong, and it was just tearing him up and that he wanted to *die*. My son's psychiatrist stated, "This man doesn't need to be in their lives, here's a piece of paper stating this, and I will testify in court to that affect." Sam never did play mind games with our daughter, partly because she's such a high achiever and partly because he just treated her as his little princess. However, she's of an age now where she has become aware *on her own* what her dad's traits are, and who he *really* is. She's currently engaged to be married and because I trailblazed in my selection. She has been wise in her choice of a young man to marry, and his family has passed the tests as well! She has elected not to have her dad give her away at her wedding.

The kids truly strengthened my decision to get out of my abusive marriage just by my seeing how it was affecting them. For a long time, I was staying in the marriage *because of them*; I then realized that I needed *out* of the marriage *because of them*. I have never regretted getting out of my abusive marriage. My kids were affected by my marriage to Sam in lots of negative ways, but now they are survivors, and they're able to find fun in very dark places—like I can now. Their friends would be overwhelmed or just cave in if they were to face circumstances like my kids endured—my kids know how to live.

Things haven't just gotten better all at once. I relied heavily on my pastor's wife, another lady at our church, a male cousin, and my mother for support and guidance throughout the breakup of my marriage. After that, I became active in my church's singles group—and that was quite an adjustment! I remained single for five years. I began to notice certain traits in men that were frightening to me. I got to a point where I had to re-think, regroup, and I said to myself, "If I remarry, I don't want to marry *you, you,* or *you!*" I learned while dating to look at what I was attracted to in a man and what was healthy, and what was not. I decided to start up a blog that selective supportive friends could read; I would put out humorous horror stories with dating warning alerts! My friends would laugh because I would always start the blog with, "Well, he *seemed* like a nice guy *and then...*"

There is one guy that I dated who I distinctly remember telling me: "The reason I've been divorced for eleven years and not remarried is that I am picky." We went to a restaurant and I ordered tacos. As we were visiting, I apparently picked up my shredded cheese with my fingers and placed it on my fork to eat. This guy looked at me and in a very creepy, soft voice said, "Did you see what you just did?" I softly said back, "No." The guy slowly told me, "You picked up that cheese, put it on your fork, and then you ate it!" I calmly said, "Well, I'm sorry." I then placed my hand under the table booth so I wouldn't do it again; but inadvertently we got to talking and I did it again! "You did it again!" he said, and he just dropped his fork as he watched me, he asked for the check. The date was over and he was done. I thought to myself, *and you were going to meet my kids?!* Not. By the time Mr. Right showed up (my current husband, Mike) I suspected *he* was normal!

Mike had moved back into our hometown. I actually met him through my parents. Mike had been working part-time at our church, and my dad had given him my email address as a referral saying that I might be able to help him find a full-time job. My dad had never in his life ever endorse a candidate for a relationship for me, but he had felt that it would be a good match—so he gave him my email address. On our first date, Mike offered to take me to the same restaurant that I had gone to with the guy who had the *picking-up the cheese with my hands* issue. So, I thought to myself, *Well, let's just get this test over with, real quick.* I ordered tacos, we started talking, and I did my cheese thing, and Mike didn't miss a beat; it was *all* good! But, what I didn't know was that two of my blog friends just happened to be in the restaurant. They stopped at our table, greeted us, looked at my plate and snorted out the door laughing! I then had to tell Mike my taco date story, which he thought was *hilarious* and then said, "So, I passed the test, right?" After dinner we headed out to a coffee shop and we talked for five hours. It was just totally different; he didn't mind my parents, my children, or the dog—because I scared a lot of guys that way!

Mike came from a Christian family. Mike's father was a pastor, but his father just never presented the gospel; he was legalistic. Mike's father ended up having an affair with a woman that was half Mike's age, fathered a child with her, and married her after divorcing Mike's mother. Mike's parents were married forty-three years. During that very same time frame, Mike found out that his own wife of thirteen years was having an affair, and *he* got a divorce. They had no children because Mike's wife didn't want to have children. Mike feels an extra bond with his mother (after both of their spouses' had affairs) because they went through such a heart-wrenching time together. Mike and his mother didn't accept salvation until after they left the church Mike's father pastored.

I first struggled with *if* I should trust Mike or not; he was just so normal despite his traumatic background. I kept waiting for stuff to just crawl out. I finally told him of my concern with trusting him—as to whether he was normal or not—and he said, "What you see is what you get, and the only way I know how to be is normal." We're not identical in our personalities, but we're *secure* in our positions; that's what makes it *fun*, we balance one another. Mike allows me to be me; he has not attempted to change who I am. Sam was always annoyed by my music; Mike doesn't mind my singing or my being musical at all. We both enjoy having a sense of humor and sometimes we both just bust out laughing! We have been married nine years now, and my daughter has asked *Mike* to give her away at her wedding. Mike's a law enforcement officer. I currently have two years of college and continue to take college courses; I work as a business analyst. I'm at a great place in my life, and it's because I did a one-eighty degree turn!

In going through all of the abuse, I had to define *who* I was in ways that I never ever had to do before. I feel like I didn't know myself well enough when I got married and I really hadn't lived long enough to know that the world is a lot bigger than my hometown—I found out! I no longer have to cautiously and pathetically figure out when I'm going to stand or sit or when I won't. I now tell women that when the person who is supposed to love you the most treats you wrong, it does very bad things inside of you. It's also important to realize that in a relationship you have to be your own cheerleader. It's okay to say to yourself, "I did a good job," or "Oh, by golly, look what *I* did!" The abuse messes you up inside in ways that you don't realize how bad its messed with you until you get into a healthy relationship.

When I was married to Sam, I would think for days as to how I was going to start a difficult conversation; I stressed over how I was going to present it to him. While newly married to Mike, I approached him with a concern and he just talked to me like a regular person and said, "Yeah, this is a hard thing. Let's figure it out." I didn't realize how many "eggshells" I had been walking on until I interacted with my parents after the divorce or after I conversed with Mike. The fact that they didn't put up a fight when I asked something of them was a new revelation to me. When you're in abnormal for so long—you forget what normal is. Having an abusive spouse is unnecessary pain—that is hard. The victim *can't* fix it; her spouse has to do that. Our pastor says that you can either learn by precept or pain; it's a choice. I live an easy, care-free life now with *no* "eggshells." Mike and I have our backs; before, I had to have my own back!

PART II

RECONCILIATION ADVISOR VS. THE PROFESSIONAL

The Reconciliation Advisor (R.A.)
THERE ARE A NUMBER of well-meaning, in-good-faith advisors out in the world that have a goal to reconcile the marriage institution at all costs. I call this type of good-intentioned advisor a "Reconciliation Advisor" (R.A.). Unfortunately, more often than not, these are advisors that are *not* well-advised on *how* to work with victims of abuse. Their lack of farsightedness leads them to a boundary violation with the victim. In essence, the R.A. is *not* being prudent about his exploitation of the victim. Sadly, our society and a number of R.A.s are anxious to identify what's wrong with the victim because if they can't find fault in her, they have to face the truth that any woman (their friend, mother, and female relatives) can become a victim of abuse. A

R.A. who expends energy on looking for what's wrong with this woman in his office (the victim) is biased in his ability to help her and automatically becomes an ally to the abuser.

Paradoxically, what is happening from the beginning when a victim seeks help from a R.A. is that the R.A. joins in with the victim's and abuser's unrealistic goal of restitution. The R.A. offers the prospect of restoring the marriage, which rewards the R.A. in feeling that he can fix the marriage, but in an abusive relationship, this is merely a magical healing intention. A R.A. leads with an attitude of the victim having to adapt, such as in assimilation, which is good for cultural adaptation but not for an abusive marriage. When a victim discloses how very bad things are for her at home—they *really* are! To work hand-in-glove and be in cahoots with the victim or abuser is an ethical dilemma. The goal to mend the abusive marriage is actually a trespassing of boundaries on behalf of the R.A. It is the R.A. who desires to restore the marriage, and therefore boundaries are crossed by ignoring the sobering reality that the safety and empowerment of the victim comes first.

Granting special favor, such as agreeing on a reconciliation goal with the victim and abuser, only brings the couple to an irresponsible level. The victim is not responsible for the grim abuse that has been done to her, but she is indeed responsible for working on not tolerating any more abuse. Doing this responsible work in her life is what will lead her to safety and strengthen her to a level of empowerment. It is totally up to the victim to reassert her authority as an individual with dignity. An abuser who enters a session with a R.A. and his victim is at his best composure and does not show his couldn't-care-less attitude; that is strictly reserved for the victim after the session. A R.A. needs to recognize that the victim who is sitting in the same session as her abuser is fearful that when she leaves his office, her abuser's tone will get to a boiling point, which will then turn his yelling

RECONCILIATION ADVISOR VS. THE PROFESSIONAL

into an unabated rage. A victim sitting quietly in an abusive marriage counseling session is not a sign that the marriage is worthy of reconciling. In victim abuse trauma, absence of evidence is not evidence of absence.

For a victim, seeking help is a *great risk* that is best used as an individual session. An individual session can offer safety options. Follow-up individual sessions can provide an opportunity for her to learn how to take responsibility for commanding respect. As an R. A., you need to know that the victim's heart in front of you is hemorrhaging from her abuser's emotional and/or physical mistreatment. She's seeking you for relief from her pain. Won't you assist her by acknowledging her bleeding heart and leading her into safety?

A R.A. needs to beware of the underlying expectations that are the true counseling goals when the abuser and victim meet with him. It is not like the inner desires of the abuser and the victim have vanished. The abuser's goal is to coercively control the victim, and the victim's goal is to *resist* his abusive control. Regardless of the abuser promising to stop being forceful and controlling, his promise comes with unspoken manipulative conditions; one of them is that in return, the victim will give up her autonomy. A R.A. has to realize that as long as the abuser has not relinquished his authoritarian dominance of the victim, the threat of his abuse is still realistic. A victim that is told to reconcile with her controlling spouse is being sent home to an eternal, abusive treadmill.

A R.A. doesn't focus on the serious moral principles being violated through the relationship that the abuser has set for the victim. A R.A. must come to grips with the fact that an abuser chooses to ignore moral conscience in the marital relationship. Therefore, change from an abusive pattern cannot be expected by simply reuniting the couple. The reason an abuser relies on no moral conscience is that if he didn't, then he would have to submit to the appropriate guilt for abusing his spouse. Some R.A.s use religious principles in their reconciliation approach. The R.A. suggests for the abuser to confess the sin of abuse to God and the victim and to seek genuine restitution with God, the victim, and others that he has hurt through his abuse. The problem is that most abusers choose not to own up to their habitual abusive behavior and instead elect not to confess their sin. If they do, unfortunately, it is not with a sincere repentant heart—electing an unrepentant conscience. Stopping his abusive actions is a standard that an abuser spurns; this, in turn, de-activates his moral conscience and responsibility. An abuser has no moral compass.

Sometimes, a R.A. who bases his reconciliation approach as a religious-based intervention wants to keep a victim (especially if she's an expectant mother) from breaking up the family. The victim can potentially be in a state of traumatized thinking and may be considering an abortion along with her abuser's wishes. She may be petrified of being abused throughout her pregnancy and may fear the fate of her unborn child. Obviously, this is an incomprehensible idea when in fact an abortion would terminate the unborn child's life prematurely. At this stage of her victimization, she *cannot* think clearly and is under the power of her abuser. A R.A. must be *aware* of the abuser's lack of moral conscience and focus on the professional's role, which is to help save two lives—the victim and her unborn child. When a R.A. prefers to proceed with reconciliation because it's the practical thing to do, he fails to meet the needs of the victim and her unborn child. By sending the victim back to the abuser, he is returning her to her place of desertion.

Yes, there is the client's right to self-determination, but a traumatized victim is not operating out of self-determination; she's basing her decision on fear of her abuser. It would be an advantage for a pregnant victim to be referred to a pregnancy center that offers a free ultrasound so that she can see and hear the baby's heartbeat. Eighty-five percent of women who see their baby through a sonogram change their mind about aborting their baby; additionally, five more percent of women who hear the heartbeat change their mind. Exposing a victim to viewing her unborn child not only saves the victim's state of Spirit, Mind, and Body, but the baby's life as well (six results).

The traumatized victim of abuse that has presented herself in your office today is (in her own being) a victim of soul-murder. She does not need a R.A. to return her to her abuser who has destroyed her ability to sense basic human trust. In some cases, the victim has been raped by her abuser. It's not possible to provide dignified and respectful care or to advocate for the victim if she's unable to disclose her rape in front of her abuser. The victim comes in despair; she could use some compassion and needs a professional to commiserate with her regarding the injustices that have been done to her. She does not need a R.A. to exculpate her abusive husband by sending her back for more injuries to the remainder of herself.

Emotional, spiritual, economic, sexual, and physical abuses invariably have severe, sometimes lifelong consequences for the victim—if not treated. Relationship abuse is stored in the Spirit, Mind, and Body, which can later be directed by the victim at others. Alternatively, the victim can turn that abuse on her own self, leading to depression, substance abuse, or other emotional illnesses and ultimately leading to an early death through accidents or suicide. This is a result of the denial of the *truth* (suppressed cruelty), which can interfere with and block the body's emotional vital functions and biological task of preserving life. When a R.A. plants the idea that the victim must honor her abusive spouse, this rests on a destructive foundation of attaching the victim to her tormentor. This recommendation, *if* the victim adheres to it, manifests into a masochistic behavioral pattern for herself, which can take the form of severe trauma through having been led to her own mental and/or physical destruction. Both a R.A. and a professional can benefit from a refresher study on the Abuser Profile and Victim Characteristics discussed in Volume I Part II and III of the *Overcoming Abuse: Embracing Peace* encyclopedic guidebook. A helper must know by heart the abuser profile, the reasons he won't change, and the victim characteristics that propel the dynamics of the abusive relationship—which is why she stays.

Once a victim is offered the accompaniment of a supportive helper that is willing to *understand* and live through her fear of her abuser, she can then gradually start to break off her destructive attachment to the abuser. The positive, *hopeful* response of her Spirit, Mind, and Body will not be long in coming; her healthy communications will develop and become more comprehensible. She will cease to express victim symptoms. It is at this time that the victim comes to a realization that her past non-supportive helpers have deceived her because reconciliation actually precludes the healing of her wounded Spirit, Mind, and Body; it restricts, and eventually obstructs her complete recovery. A reconciliation approach can never dispel the victim's compulsion to return and repeat the same pattern over and over again, a finding that can be traced back to all of the statistics on the cycle of abuse.

My bringing to light the misleading idea of the theory of reconciliation is not to be equated with refusing to recognize the sanctity of the institution of marriage or with my having a wholesale rejection of forgiveness. On the contrary, it is because I respectfully uphold the fundamental matrimonial values of commitment, respect, trust, integrity, and responsibility that I advocate with loyalty to these vows for the awareness of the denial of truths that are considered self-evident and have been empirically substantiated in all studies of marital abuse. The and her damaged and sometimes destroyed trust levels can only offer the professional fragmented phases of doubt with intermittent trust and suspicion that he will not listen to her, either (and perhaps may even deceive her). Some victims attribute the abuser's ulterior motives to the professional. Work with the victim, at this point, needs to focus on *how* the abuser has altered her relational style. The victim is in need of recognizing and accepting that she fears being re-victimized and is scared of being unable to protect herself.

The labels of marital communication problems and incompatibility, and even the diagnosing of the victim and blaming *her* for the marital problems is often a part of a R.A. *mislabeling*. This diagnostic mislabeling is reinforced by society and even research that has attempted to identify *personality traits* that might predispose the victim to engage in abusive relationships. This research has not focused on the abuser's persuasive tactics that might engage a victim in an abusive relationship, but instead it focuses on the victim's role. The research has *not* been an inquiry of the abuser's violence and his behavior that he's responsible for; it has been about the victim's contributing traits that lead her to her own victimization. While males and females both are prone to develop mental illnesses that predispose them as being more vulnerable to abuse, most research indicates that victims have demonstrated no evidence of mental illness prior to entering into an abusive relationship.

There are some victims that, during patient intake, have been labeled with the theory of "learned helplessness" as a part of the assessment evaluation. Learned helplessness studies posit that when subjects were repeatedly maltreated and couldn't escape, the subjects stopped trying to avoid the maltreatment and acted helpless in changing the situation; when opportunity to escape was made available, the subjects did not take action. The victim is assigned this label due to her apparent passive and helpless portrayal of how she has handled her relationship(s). This may be accurate for a patient that is being victimized due to her acute powerlessness, low self-esteem, a social upbringing that rewarded her helpless stance, and other dynamics that *do not* include abuse trauma. A victim of abuse has had to learn *not to* take action because most of her actions are balked at, foiled, and impeded through the use of the abuser's tactics. For her, it is more a case of being so fearful and entrapped in the abusive relationship that a sense of hopelessness sets in with the thinking that there is no solution to this problem. The abuser has schemed to successfully get the victim to submit to vulnerability and hopelessness by programming her mind to think that any action of her *own* individuality is acting-up and *she* pays dearly for asserting herself! If the chronic stress is removed and the option of a safe escape with victim trauma assistance is offered, most victims do not submit to what appears to be the phenomenon of learned helplessness.

A cautionary word about Christian R.A.s who contribute to victim *learned helplessness* via counseling, writing, or guidance; by labeling the abuser with a diagnosis. This is especially true when they label the abuser as an "addict." Have you ever noticed that those who speak or write about an abuser being "addicted" to a vice (and abuse *is* a vice) are actually re-victimizing the victim by labeling the abuser and assigning *her* the responsibility of taking the leadership (victim) role of "fighting" against her abuser's "addiction" (which is destroying her and their family). The R.A. allows the abuser to switch his role from being a godly leader and instead approves for the victim to become her spouse's primary caretaker; her role now is to take care of his misdeeds (sin). It's a role-reversal that hands over her spouse's spiritual leadership (which God did not assign to her) as she is encouraged to go to battle and combat his "addiction" (sin).

RECONCILIATION ADVISOR VS. THE PROFESSIONAL

Notice the abuse is not called what it is. The abuser no longer has the selfish sin problem which he has repeatedly exhibited against his wife, it's no longer a traumatizing vice against her; it's an "addiction." The truth is that a vice has never been defined as an "addiction." The term *addiction* has actually been re-created by those in denial of an abuser's and victim's role and their enablers—as a substitute term for—*abuse*. The word addiction has replaced the definition of a vice which in reality is an immoral act or by definition in the English language in plain terms is, "an evil habit or practice." A vice (sin) is a choice not an addiction. The word vice means immoral conduct, depraved or degrading behavior; which is the behavior an abuser engages in.

R.A.s don't call abuse (pornography, gambling, and/or other infidelity impulsive and compulsive behavioral acts) "depraved or degrading behavior" toward the victim; instead they rename the abusive acts as an "addiction" which some victim wives are willing to tolerate and accept when the R.A. assigns them such a role *in the name of love and marriage:* the role of working to heal the abuser's "addiction." A R.A., who joins the abuser in undervaluing his wife by minimizing and undermining his traumatic abuse of her, empowers the abuser; reinforces his abuse, by calling his amoral disrespectful behaviors toward her an "addiction."

The abuser can now take control of the counseling session or as a group leader lead other "addicts" (abusers) into recovery; not acknowledging the self-entitled abuse (sin) he has imposed upon the victim and their family. The abuser may make amends with some apologies simulating repentance; but in general it is with the expectation that the victim is to ignore the damage he has caused. If the abuser has a personal sin problem with obsessive compulsive and impulsive behaviors it is *his* sin problem to fix. God has never assigned anyone, as an act of *love;* to fix someone else's sin problem. When attempts are made to fix another's sin problem; he may refrain from sin, but since it was not his own initiative, admission, conviction, and repenting desire to stop sinning, there's always a possibility that he will return to that sin.

Sending a wife home to assist her spouse in fixing his "addiction" (sin) problem is taking God's role. God's the only One Who can help the abuser fix his sin problem. God never declared in His Word that one of the duties of marriage is to fix the spouse's "addiction." Choosing to abuse (a vice) is not an addiction—it is a sin. Sin is not an "in sickness and in health" problem. Sin is a willful deliberate violation of God's principles against Him, oneself, and another. Furthermore, calling the spouse's abuse an "addiction" converts his immoral behaviors into acts that are depersonalized and the burden is transferred to the victim as *her problem* to resolve. This justifies the abuse and her victim role as legitimate, because it is an "addiction" and injurious traumatic abuse toward her and the family are not to be addressed, but the abuser's recovery as an "addict" is. The R.A. focuses on the spouse's neurobiological addiction but not on a neurological test to assess for her traumatic brain injury (from his emotional and/or other abuse of her).

Assigning a victim the spiritual role of helping her spouse to govern his addiction (sin) plays into her vulnerable low self-esteem disempowering her from speaking out against her abusive maltreatment and sustaining the already internalized trauma as a part of her being. It is the R.A.'s responsibility to validate the victim's abuse and address the abuser's vice as *his sin*, and *not* the victim's role to resolve. In James 1:14-15 *sin* is described as being tempted by one's own desires by being enticed; which then gives birth to sin. Frankly, it is written that sin happens as a result of our own desires; that we are enticed and tempted by our own lure. But, that passage also warns us that having that desire, enticement, and temptation does not mean that we have to give in to those thoughts and feelings (desires). The verse explains that it's only when those desires are conceived and we give birth to them; that we then engage in and commit sin.

In John 8:11 when Christ spoke to the woman accused of adultery (a vice); He first above all, prevented and protected her from being abused—stoned. The woman was vulnerable, Christ prioritized her safety. Then, He commanded her to *go and sin no more*. That command about sin is very clear. It was not just about what not-to-do and what to-do regarding *her* sin. Christ essentially told her to say *no* to sin and to *stop* being tempted into her own desires; to *stop* the enticement from turning into sin against Him, her, and others. The same instructions are there for all of us. Christ's instructions as to *what-to-do* about sin have not changed in modern society. Sin was forbidden during biblical times as it is today.

The R.A. misses the mark on abuse trauma, safety, and Christ's definition of and command about sin, by labeling the abuser with a diagnosis. Christ did not call immoral acts of sin an "addiction." He did not excuse sin by saying, "I know sin is a persistent obsessive compulsive immoral behavior that you're addicted to and over which you have no power or choice." Christ did not say, "You have a sexual addiction." He called sexual and other vices listed in the Bible—sin. An abuser welcomes a R.A. and the opportunity to be self-entitled by calling his abuse an "addiction" over which he has no power especially in the presence of whom he considers his less entitled wife and children. When the woman committed adultery—Christ called it sin and He did not disempower the woman. Rather—He empowered her—through His instructions "'go and sin no more'" which emphatically let the woman and all of us know that we have a choice and power over sin.

Professionals Prioritize Safety

It is a victim's vulnerability and inability for the victim to help her own self to safety that renders a professional responsible for the initial intervention to be a development of a Safety Escape Plan (SEP). Victims usually seek professional help when they are in a state of crisis. These victims find themselves in a vicious cycle with a fear of losing their life and their children's lives and anger toward the abuser, along with a fear of losing the abuser! Your role is to gently lead the victim to safety and peace, albeit losing the abuser. Studies of victims have established that they usually underestimate their own risk for safety. A good rule of thumb is to measure the victim's level of risk for safety; listen for or ask about the abuser's type of safety threats (if she doesn't talk about her safety).

It's important to identify which types of abuse the victim is suffering from for the purpose of developing a treatment plan as well as for strategically designing the SEP to suit her particular abuse trauma. Even if there's no apparent physical abuse, there is still an emotional safety problem, and "no contact" is required in order for the victim to overcome her abuse. Without expanding further on the subject of the various abuses (there are seven types of abuse with comprehensive definitions in Volume I Part I), it's of utmost importance for a helper to be well-versed on types of abuses, the traumatic impact, and the consequences for the victim. Review the no contact rule with her; remind her that no contact means a clean break and the end of *all* communication with the abuser. Remember that she has been carrying on, but in a trance-like, automaton state. It's as if she's been on life-support tubes, and she fears that the abuser will pull the plug or keep her plugged in just to have control of her life. Offer her your supportive protection. Keep calm to reduce the victim's anxiety and flooding of fearful thoughts. Make the evaluation as simple as possible so as not to overwhelm the victim with unnecessary paperwork. Use the KIS-S method: Keep it Simple-Safety.

Most professionals' offices already have specific assessment forms that inquire about the family's social life and history of trauma; these assessments include current evaluation for suicidal or homicidal ideation. The assessment forms are useful in providing lead questions to diagnose the victim's and the family's current physical and emotional status. As has been established, abuse is at serious risk for homicide or suicide mental health diagnoses and is not a function of everyday marriage problems. As such, abuse requires intervention in order for the victim to reduce or eliminate her symptoms, improve her functioning, and restore her quality of living. As noted, identifying an abuse victim requires more than your observations of the characteristics or waiting for the victim to come forward to describe her symptoms. In order to identify a victim of abuse, you have to ask *specific* questions about her thoughts, feelings, and behaviors in a reliable way so that you can assess if victimization exists and not incorrectly identify abuse. An effective way of asking significant questions is by administering a questionnaire that identifies specific victim symptoms.

When a victim remains in a quandary about whether she's being abused and is uncertain as to whether she's safe, have her take a moment to answer the *Adult Victim Domestic Violence Assessment Tool* (provided in the Resources section of this book). This tool was designed by the *Denton County Friends of the Family* to evaluate safety and at-risk status, to assist the victim in decision-making, and to connect her to advocacy. The assessment tool can direct the professional or case worker to provide information about the potential availability of Crime Victim's Compensation (CVC) if the victim reports the abuse to the police and or secures a protective order. The tool can be used to assess strengths and needs and to guide staff in treatment planning and case management. Overall, the tool provides a preliminary safety evaluation for the victim and professional.

A safety risk to listen for is what the victim has heard as threats from the abuser. The chances greatly increase for the death of the victim if the abuser has indeed stated, "I'm going to kill you" (and/or the children). An abuser in this category is usually feeling astronomically low about his own self and is aiming to make the victim to feel in the same way about her own self. It is even more difficult for her to make decisions about her own life and her children's lives if she's feeling particularly low about herself. If he includes, "I'm going to kill *myself after* I kill you" (and/or the children), the risk of death for the victim is even greater with this type of abusive threat. This is because some abusers have the attitude that, "If I can't have *all* of you, neither I nor anyone else will!"

A Woman Abuse Screening Tool (WAST, Sample in Resources) can also be used as a reliable, validated method of identifying victim and family abuse. The tool is purposely designed to be simple but with direct, open-ended questions so as not to overwhelm the victim; yet, it has the prompts for her to reply with a response other than a "yes" or "no" answer. The open-ended questions are phrased as statements in order to provide the victim the freedom to have a voice clarifying what is true and not true in her circumstances; therefore, it helps to obtain a full, informative response.

This tool is effective when abuse is suspected because it is short and allows for the victim to be comfortable with the questions asked in the form. For some victims, their symptoms may appear subtle as they are so good at covering up their victimization and denying their abuse, an act which may seem plausible. A victim screening tool eliminates the guesswork in identifying a victim who may be experiencing symptoms of abuse. The tool helps to identify the victim earlier than just waiting for the victim to process and eventually self-disclose her at-risk abuse. Over time, the initial screening tools are also useful in tracking treatment progress. In time, the victim herself will be able to monitor and track her own symptoms as you both work together to circumvent her victim role. From the initial screening tools, the victim can set treatment goals, and at some point, she can look back and now celebrate her self-efficacy in her spiritual, emotional, and physical accomplishments.

It is especially important to also periodically evaluate the victim's and her children's level and stage of anger in the relationship with the abuser. Morality issues will have to be dealt with later through the therapeutic process so that she can absolve herself of any coerced moral behaviors the abuser enforced upon her, but there are also moral areas that have to be immediately evaluated regarding safety and consequences if the victim and/or children take revenge upon the abuser. I have had several patients disclose their plan to hurt their abuser.

One victim stated that she was fed up with her spouse's abuse and planned to use one of his hunting rifles to shoot him if he ever raped her again. She *hysterically* cried as she said, "All I ever did was get pregnant during our honeymoon, and we mutually agreed that after we both graduated from law school, I would be a stay-at-home mom. Ever since then, he has come home and acted like a hostile prosecuting attorney toward me, and last night, he raped me, and I can't take it anymore!" Another scenario involved an adolescent girl who shared her despair as she had continuously watched her pregnant mother being abused by her father. She proceeded to state angrily that she planned on placing rat poison in his favorite vegetable soup the next time he attacked her mother. Taking the law into their own hands (premeditated) will have to be processed and hopefully dissuaded through the victims' own moral decision-making. Ethical concerns here warrant advising the victim of the professional's responsibility to report to the proper authorities whenever a patient is a danger to herself or others.

Safety is not all about the patient and their family. It is a common professional practice as well. It is important that the professional have an already-established safety plan for himself and his practice. Maintaining a safe work environment is a must during the work with victims and even after the case is closed. Well-developed policies, procedures, signed consent forms, and emergency safety plans have to be in place at the professional's practice if a victim becomes aggressive and/or her abuser shows up and creates an out-of-control environment. A professional is always at the risk of the abuser whenever he is working with family violence. A professional therapist knows how to protect and take care of himself, his patients, and his staff. Therapists are trained to be on top of Secondary Traumatic Stress (the emotional impact on the therapist while listening to the firsthand trauma experiences of the victims). They're aware that the necessary act of listening and being exposed to the victims' trauma can lead to their own moral injury and PTSD symptoms, which, if left unsupervised, can compromise their professional functioning and ultimately affect their mental health and well-being.

Until a victim of abuse has fully developed an articulate contingency plan for her safety and has actively demonstrated her capability to follow through, she is still *at risk* for returning to be abused or her abuser returning to abuse her. Whenever a victim declines the option of a SEP, and she has disclosed a danger to herself and others, I have her sign her medical chart to indicate that she has opted *not* to implement a SEP. A victim in the initial stages of counseling is still very quick to blame herself for the abuse she has endured. This is coupled with the fact that the abuser states that, "I can't help it" when she reports his abuse to the counselor (but yet is able to have self-control at work or in other relationships).

RECONCILIATION ADVISOR VS. THE PROFESSIONAL

A victim and abuser should seek counseling separately; individual and group counseling for her, abuser program for him. It is not advised that the abuser seek individual counseling, as an abuser's program is strategically designed to confront and treat his coercive control of the victim. If the victim is unable to safely or financially afford counseling, it is paramount that she secures a trustworthy person who may be willing to be available to her as a supportive listener and can guide her with ideas for finding resources to get help. It's important for her to ventilate her hurt feelings; suppressing her painful wounds becomes detrimental. Festering injured feelings in her heart will gradually contaminate her mind and eventually poison her entire being—who she is, who she becomes, and what becomes of her.

Once the victim understands that in order to establish her safety, she will *not* be able to include her abuser in her counseling sessions, she may *still* struggle with his invisible presence anyway. Even if the victim has made the decision to separate or end her relationship with her abuser, she will intermittently be interrupted in her therapeutic process by his presence in her mind. The victim has difficulty adapting to the idea that the abuser is no longer in her present world—even after weeks and months of being separated from him. She continues to have a sense that he is still around her being. All the more, after a period of time has passed, her relational world has a tendency to include him in her atmosphere. The victim has to be directed to work on her mindful thinking as it is the only strategy that will keep her abuser from working in her thoughts. The task of the professional to continually redirect the victim to her safety does not end until she overcomes her abuse.

Establishing a Safety Escape Plan with the Victim
Some victims have not had the strength or privacy to call a shelter or domestic violence program to receive assistance with

developing a Safety Escape Plan (SEP). If the victim is willing to learn how to develop a Safety Escape Plan, it is your responsibility to guide her through the steps of creating a SEP. Encourage her to develop a SEP for the sake of her life and that of her children if she has them. Don't allow her anxiety or fear to say, "I'll think about it." Remind her that there's nothing to think about when it comes to her safety except about having a plan to escape her abuse—and that you can help her develop that plan today.

Even if she doesn't have the energy to create a SEP, reassure her that you will help her through the process and that together you will develop a safety plan so that she can escape her abusive lifestyle (even if she does not have a sense of what her future as an *Overcomer* of abuse holds). Teach her self-talk and to refuse to do nothing about her safety. Ask her to tell herself that a SEP is a tool to equip her against her abuse danger so that she can have a SEP ready to use. The victim can be encouraged to protect herself with additional back-up support through pre-arranged persons that can intervene once the escape plan goes into effect. This process could be making use of assistance from a shelter or asking for the intervention of a police officer, a nearby neighbor, friend, or relative.

The SEP is a combined formula that is used based on the variety of victim cases and the information that has been gathered on victim abuse. Abusive relationships have the same dynamics but varied circumstances. Not every safety strategy applies to every victim; options and flexibility are made available. If there are children involved in this abusive relationship, strategically design her plan to safeguard the risk for their safety, too. Incorporate *all* safety precaution elements for herself into the plan of escape to take the children with her. Connect the victim with a women's crisis center hotline and have her use the counselor's suggestions in setting up additional strategies to safely get herself and the children to a shelter or designated location.

RECONCILIATION ADVISOR VS. THE PROFESSIONAL

There's a high risk that her abuser will attempt to harm the children, manipulate them to betray her, or use the judicial system against her; this issue needs to be considered as a part of the safety planning process.

Explain to the victim how the SEP will help her to separate her confusion about the abuse and abuser and give her clarity of mind about a safety vision for her life. Remind her that developing a SEP requires mindful thinking and that being mindful will increase her courage to drive her life in the direction of her safety. Reassure her trust in your assistance with whatever challenges she has with developing the SEP, and remind her that all victims have to take a faith leap with a SEP if they are going to experience a safe escape.

Leaving the *victim* role and stepping out into the *Overcomer* role is, for a victim, like walking onto a tightrope—there is no way she can trust that she will not fall off without holding on to faith, but as she steadies herself throughout the process, she gradually steps across the finish line. There are some absolutes for victim safety that a helper must make known to the victim contemplating creating a SEP. If the victim and her children are being physically abused, she does not have an option—other than to create a SEP. Lead the victim to focus on the SEP and overcoming her abuse, *not* on her fears of having a SEP or feeling like she is betraying/breaking her marital trust in her relationship. This is where you are to remind her that this is not a trusting marital relationship—it is an abusive relationship. That realization deems it necessary to create a SEP. Provide the insight that it is only those victims that take the SEP route that now live abuse-free lives. Discourage any thoughts or plans to run away as opposed to following an intentional SEP. Inform her that abuse only escalates when a victim attempts to run from the abuser. Promote the healthy approach to mindfully strategizing instead of an emotional escape with nowhere to go. It is not a safe approach to escape in the midst of the abuser's explosive threats.

The only way to escape the abuse is to confront the abuse, admit the abuser has been abusive, and work out a strategic SEP to overcome the abuse. Have her push through writing out her SEP because she is pushing toward her *Overcomer* vision. She may pause to think that she's going to lose her home; suggest that she think of it as like she's losing a material possession and gaining her new *Overcomer* life. Whatever a victim tries to convince herself of or others about managing her abusive circumstances, the trauma of abuse only increases without a resolve and intervention. The ray of hope is that although she has been enslaved, with a purposed, judiciary, strategic plan, she can be set free. The helper is there to outline a safety plan for her particular circumstances and to guide her into finding a specific plan which will cause her to find her own safety path. Remind her that no matter how difficult her circumstances become, she is never to discuss her safety plan with her abuser because it is impossible to communicate about safety with an abuser. It is not an option for a victim to receive her abuser's understanding or consent to leave if he gets abusive—abusers may feign empathy, but at the end of the day, the SEP would be used against the victim at exacerbated levels of anger and control.

Let the victim know that designing a SEP is a solid commitment to her safety. While she's working on developing her SEP, guide her to avoid being pulled in by her fantasies of reconciliation with the abuser—allow her to see the realistic error in those thoughts and help her to keep a strong grip on the truth about the relationship. Identify and have her consider the abusive incidents that led her to this point of a SEP; they are her wake-up call. Perhaps she has been engrossed in her abusive cycle, but the most recent abusive incident has scared her into a rude awakening about her abuse. Although it's unfortunate that the victim has to experience a devastating episode or hit rock bottom in her abusive relationship in order to do something about stopping the abuse, reassure her that there's a positive in the negative and that the positive is that her breaking point will lead her to the path of an *Overcomer*. Instill hope in her heart that a SEP will offer her an opportunity to leave her life of suffering at the hands of her abuser and that it will bring connections to resources which will restore her peace of mind and support her *Overcomer* goals.

A victim always receives the idea that her unique self-identity will be restored after she escapes her abusive relationship with such relief. However, it's important that she is mindful that she is the only one who can restore her individual self through the experience of seeking help and resources for her abuse trauma and the act of finding them. The helper's validation of her abuse is important, but the victim must equally recognize that she is living in danger, that she does not deserve to be abused but deserves to be respected, and that there is a better, peaceful life to live.

There are abusers who demand out of the relationship or abandon the relationship on one or more projected grounds. Regardless of who initiates to end the abusive relationship, a SEP still has to be developed. An abuser's characteristic profile does not change just because he terminates the relationship. He's an abuser; it's in his usual demeanor that he reverses and distorts interactions with the victim. When the victim finally accepts his desire to break up the relationship, he still has the desire to take vengeance toward her for ending the relationship (as if it were her idea). The abuser will return in person with his projective identification or via some form of distorted communication and complain about what the victim has done to destroy the relationship and about how deeply she has hurt him.

Overcoming abuse always starts with the victim seeking help. When a victim reaches out for help, the steps to healing begin to happen in her life. Have her take that blind faith step to believe that this is a good day for a breakthrough in resolving her abuse—even if she's unable to see the limitless positive outcome of drawing up her SEP. If you are a Christian helper (whether or not you know that she's a believer), offer to pray out loud for her as she embarks upon the development of her Safety Escape Plan. The worst that can happen is that she will decline your offer, but this may change over time as her trust of you increases. Initiating prayer, on the other hand, can begin that trusting bond with you as her helper as she watches you bow down to seek God's assistance on her behalf. Observing your prayer of faith and humility role models to her how in the same way she can seek God's guidance. Share with her that God calls us to pray to Him (Jeremiah 33:3) and reassure her that God would never ask her to do anything ritualistic, meaningless, or purposeless. Prayer is basically a human mind reaching out to a power higher and greater than the self. Remind her that prayer will connect her to God Who knows and comprehends the desires of her heart. Praying with her encourages her to begin to see you as a part of her circle of supportive helpers. Later, she may find others like you to privately ask for specific prayers regarding her abuse. Praying aloud with her is different from saying, "I will be praying for you" because it is a visually tangible interaction that lets her know that you will help to carry her load through Jesus—and this will instill hope.

Some people find it difficult to pray aloud for someone; it may be helpful for you to begin by practicing praying aloud when you are alone in prayer with God. Then graduate to praying aloud with a colleague, friend, or brother and sister in Christ. Never compare your spoken prayers with those of others. It is the Holy Spirit who formulates our prayers. If ever you hear

RECONCILIATION ADVISOR VS. THE PROFESSIONAL

another person pray with guided fluency and perceive it as eloquence in prayer with you seeing yourself as barely uttering out efficient words, you then are accusing yourself of inadequate prayer intervention, as if another's prayers have the golden key to the door of prayer. We must each come into prayer such as God's Word expects us to: confidently and boldly, such as a child comes to his parent.

You don't have to take the role of teaching the victim *how* to pray; the Lord will teach her how to pray through His Spirit. She can trust in His ability to teach her to pray. He is an excellent Counselor. As the victim becomes comfortable with seeking God in prayer, she will find many avenues of prayer through the Bible's many snapshot images of His promises, His infinite goodness, and His power. These images of God will become imprinted in her memory recall, in her heart, and in her Spirit; she will naturally become bold in her faith and prayer. Pray with the victim whatever comes to mind as God's Spirit leads you!

"Likewise the Spirit also helps in our weaknesses. For we do not know what we should pray for as we ought, but the Spirit Himself makes intercession for us with groanings which cannot be uttered. Now He who searches the hearts knows what the mind of the Spirit *is*, because He makes intercession for the saints according to *the will of* God" (Romans 8:26-27).

The following is a basic example of a Safety Escape Plan (SEP) from an abusive relationship. More or different strategies can be added depending on the victim and her particular circumstances:

1. Purchase a prepaid cellphone (see Resources). She must always keep it on the silent setting. Program shortcut tools or voice recognition in the phone so that she will only have to dial one number to contact the police or her support resources. She must only use this phone for *all* abuse safety plan calls. Use the phone to save information such

as the addresses to your closest police station, hospital, or other sources.
2. Purchase a Post Office Box (POB) at a post office that her abuser does not frequent so that she can receive confidential mail from the women's abuse program and other support organizations. If she's unable to set up a POB, she must do whatever she can to get her mail through a trusted person.
3. Set up an email account through a library computer or trusted friend's computer.
4. Open up a bank account at a bank that the abuser does not use so she can build up funds for her use upon escaping.
5. Make duplicate photo and hard copies of *all* important documents (passport, hers and his social security cards, birth certificate, health cards, insurance policies, school records, certificates, resume, portfolio, car registration, Protective Order, photos of her abuse evidence, etc.). Also make copies of house and car keys. She must not take originals from where they are stored, or he will suspect she's leaving.
6. Hide a duffel bag (not necessarily in her home and not at a next-door neighbor's or mutual friend's home) packed with copies of documents, copies of keys, and a wallet with cash. ATM and credit cards leave tracks, so use these only with discretion. Pack travel sized toiletries, feminine products, underwear, and seasonal layered outfits; take only what is absolutely irreplaceable in sentimental value.
7. Plan where she will stay when she leaves. Friends, family, and hotels are convenient but *not* the safest due to her abuser having access to this contact information. The hotline or program for abused women will be able to provide her with information for a safer place to go to.

RECONCILIATION ADVISOR VS. THE PROFESSIONAL

8. Register (if illegal in her state) for a firearm permit to carry pepper spray.
9. She must never attempt to escape if she's under the influence of drugs or alcohol as her impairment will derail her plan.
10. If her abuser suspects that she is leaving and she believes he will become violently explosive, she must keep the door or window unlocked for fleeing and exiting quickly. She has to plan various escape routes from within her home in case her abuser catches her on her way out and becomes violent. She can use her prepaid phone to call the police and women's abuse hotline if she gets caught escaping. *If at all possible, it's best for her to leave from work or a regularly-scheduled activity.*

The victim is to always be prepared and ready to leave and put into effect her Safety Escape Plan any of the three hundred and sixty-five days a year. It is recommended that a victim have a pre-arranged understanding with a shelter or trusted out-of-town friend or family member (whom the abuser cannot contact) that when in danger, the contacts will receive a call from her. Some victims have escaped to safety at their friends' or family members' homes or high-rise residences that have twenty-four-hour security. These contacts should be those who know that she will be calling if in danger at any hour. A code or word should be set up, indicating that she's leaving and is on her way to their place of safety. Another code word may be established to notify her contact that she wants them to call the police to come to her home.

Whether she decides to use a women's shelter or friend's or family member's place of safety, it is still highly recommended that she reports the abuse and obtains a protective order to restrain her abuser from attempting to attack her at her place of safety. The police report and protective order will also serve as her documentation, which can be used in the legal process of separation/divorce/child custody.

The post escape safety plan must include being ever so careful about protecting the privacy of her residential address. Remind her that *no contact* with the abuser also means *do not* return to her former domicile (whether he's home or not) lest he track her from his home to her new home. Train her in safety savvy prevention and protection regarding important items left behind; instruct her to value herself, her safety, and her life over losing a significant item.

Some states have an Address Confidentiality Program that provides victims of family violence a confidential address to list on applications, forms, and legal records. This program can also be used to forward mail from the confidential address to the victim's temporary or new home address. A victim can apply for a confidential address through the local domestic violence, sexual assault, or victim's services office. Some victims that I have worked with have opted for requesting the judicial system to allow for a change in social security number and name change in an effort to hide from the abuser and start over with a new identity. However, there are realities and consequences with this option.

Such changes can make it increasingly difficult for the victim in the areas of employment, especially when receiving services and benefits without any prior records in her name and identifying social security number. Since most official records are filed at the courthouse, licensing bureaus, and state agencies, they are considered public information. Even when the judge seals the records, making these changes *does not deter* the abuser from purchasing the information online, computer tampering, or hacking as so many agencies nowadays post records online. There are information brokers that gather personal data on individuals in each state which they then combine into data profiles and sell.

RECONCILIATION ADVISOR VS. THE PROFESSIONAL

Even if these profiles are gathered for marketing purposes, there are limited legal restrictions that would restrain an abuser from obtaining a victim's personal profile.

The Social Security Administration is restricted in its ability to keep a victim's social security number confidential; they can't give out the number without her consent, but they have to make her information available to some federal and state government agencies. So, a victim changing her social security number or name *is not* guaranteed more protection than establishing a well-thought-out solid safety plan through a Domestic Violence Program (DVP). Most victims are safer by establishing a new job/career in another area, state, or country. However, it is *always* recommended that she consult with her attorney along with her family violence advocate at the DVP for the *best* options in *her* particular circumstances.

I have known some victims that have elected to completely vanish from their residence in order to establish their safety with the intent to be declared missing and dead and to protect themselves from the abuser through such means. Most states create their own laws for declaring someone legally dead. Generally, the missing person is presumed dead if, for a specified number of years (three or more depending on the state) significant others have not had any contact with the person (an extensive inquiry and search has been conducted) and the person has been missing without any explanation. It is easy for a victim to cover up her victimization for fear of the abuser and for the abuser to maintain a reputation as a civil citizen; for a victim vanishing without an explanation seems simpler than developing a SEP.

Nonetheless, a victim must seriously consider the consequences of totally vanishing. The repercussions of loss are too many to enumerate in this book (insurance, retirement or work pension benefits, assets, child-support, healthcare, and passport), but the basic loss of a social security number and driver's license is an essential one to consider. Sure, *it is* possible to petition in federal court that her social security number be reinstated, but the court's ruling on the long-term unexplained absence is presumption of death, and most judges will not overturn a ruling when the law has declared the person deceased. If a former victim decides that she wants to use any of her documents from her past identity in the future, a judge will not accept the victim's explanation that her life was in danger and that she needed to start her life over again away from the abuser in a safe environment. Upon returning, she is now to be declared alive. Again, have her seek legal counsel and support from an advocate at the DVP before considering leaving without an established Safety Escape Plan.

Establishing a Post-Escape Plan with the *Overcomer*
The message that the victim (and all humans) deserves to live with dignity and respect—at peace and free from fear—needs to keep being engrained into the *Overcomer*'s mindful thinking. Now that the victim has established a Safety Escape Plan while living with the abuser, she must develop a Post-Escape Safety Plan (PESP) to activate while she is separated from him. Due to the numerous victims who return to the abuser after successfully implementing and achieving positive results from their Safety Escape Plan, this is also a time (if you are a believer) to suggest that the *Overcomer* pray for her ability to maintain her no-contact with the abuser and to not break her commitment to her own and her children's safety. Here's a sample prayer of faith and reassurance of God's commitment to sustaining and providing for her needs after her escape from her abuse:

> "Father, God, what a joy it is for _____ to come to You boldly at Your throne. We praise You that through Your mercy and grace she has

successfully removed herself from the dangers of her abuse. How grateful she is that she is able to come to You *unafraid* to seek freedom from her abuse and to feel confident in Your welcoming acceptance of her as she turns to You for the non-wavering energy and strength which she needs in order to fulfill her resolve, to live her life free from abuse. Thank You that she can approach Your throne confidently knowing that You forgive any past failures, that You will answer, and that You only have unconditional love for her every need. In Christ's Merciful Name, Amen."

Recall for the victim that God's Presence is with her day by day to renew her strength and refresh her Spirit through prayer and His Word. Instruct her to create Scriptural reminders that bring to mind God's promises of protection whenever she is feeling fearful and unsafe on her phone or on sticky notes posted wherever she frequents in her home. Have her memorize the verses as affirmations which she can hide in her heart. Such as, "The fear of man brings a snare, But whoever trusts in the Lord shall be safe" (Proverbs 29:25). Help her to realize that prayer is her daily prescription, not just when she's feeling weak and thinking about returning to her abuser, but as an everyday renewal of being an *Overcomer*, replenishing her from her stressors and empowering herself through the indwelling of God's Spirit in her.

Impress upon her that prayer is one of the most amazing, inspirational forces that a human can experience. It will raise her up from the mire of fear, anxiety, self-condemnation, and her abusive bottomless pit, restore her, and bring her into the Holy Presence of God—the forgiver and the healer of all diseases. "Who forgives all your iniquities, Who heals all your diseases"

(Psalm 103:3). If she is feeling especially vulnerable and unable to pray, tell her not to get discouraged but to silently pray whenever she is ready and able to pray; in the meantime, remind her that God's Word promises that Jesus Christ our High Priest can intercede in prayer for us. Instruct her that she can ask Christ to pray to the Father for her courage, strength, and disposition to say "no" to the abuser. "Let us therefore come boldly to the throne of grace, that we may obtain mercy and find grace to help in time of need" (Hebrews 4:16).

The following are some post-escape safety strategies which are not limited to this list, but rather, have to be tailored to the new Overcomer's circumstances:

1. Before she moves out of her safety resource, she must secure an *updated* protection order on her abuser. Make multiple copies of the protection order and keep them on her person and everywhere she goes (school, work, church, gym).
2. Never walk or drive the identical routes when she travels to her places of commitment.
3. Notify her county police, neighbors, employer, co-workers, and children's school of her abuser's danger status, and provide a photo of him along with a description of the vehicle(s) he drives.
4. Have an established safety plan that if her abuser approaches her children that they will *not* speak to him. Ask them to seek the agreed upon resources for help. Provide prepaid phones for your older children and instruct them to call 911 if the abuser shows up.
5. Secure an established safety protection plan with her local police should her abuser violate her protection order.

Having a well-developed PESP will provide the *Overcomer* with confidence and established security. If she stays in her home, the only way she will feel safe (even if she has a restraining

RECONCILIATION ADVISOR VS. THE PROFESSIONAL

order) is if she changes her door locks and has a security system that contacts the police upon signaling her that the abuser is on her property. If she left with a vehicle in her name, she must change the door locks in her car.

Her abuser may return. Even if he is or she is involved in another relationship, engaged, or remarried, this does not matter to him. The research shows that the abuser doesn't change his abuse toward the victim once she terminates the relationship. Research from the National Domestic Violence Hotline shows that the average victim leaves her abuser seven times before she leaves him permanently. During the end-cycle of abuse, some victims separate, return, renew their vows, or divorce their abuser, reconcile, and remarry the abuser before the final departure.

Not all victims make a permanent decision to end their abusive relationship and to live an *Overcomer* lifestyle. Volume I Part III lists seven processes that the victim undergoes which serve as a mark that an *Overcomer* has indeed made a permanent move into an abuse-free life.

It is preemptive that a victim gets past the separation step and applies her *Overcomer* principles and new *Overcomer* characteristics as a daily practice if she's not going to be controlled by the abuser after leaving him. Volume II Part II defines and lists the *Overcomer* Principles and provides a criteria list with the *Overcomer* Characteristics. An abuser doesn't randomly stop abusing; he just changes his approach and format as to *how* and through *whom* or *what* he attempts to abuse in order to re-victimize the *Overcomer*. The abuser's weapon of return is his usual attempt to frighten the victim. However, one of the mottos of an *Overcomer*, which is derived from her *Overcomer* principles is, "Never surrender to fear." The former victim was a slave to fear—the new *Overcomer* is not.

Helping the Victim with the Here & Now

The abuser has secured his presence in her mind, such as he did when he forced his presence on her during her relationship with him. The abuser interrupts her thoughts and enters into her presence through her mind. The abuser's sense of presence in the victim's world, even after she is free from his control, is monopolizing her attention to him as he did while he was abusing her. The professional has to intervene, assisting the victim with removing this preoccupation from her new inner life and to thinking without the abuser. The confrontation of this thought process (her mind's inability to escape him) will help her to focus on this as a thought interruption and to view it as an interference keeping her from being able to move on with her life.

It would behoove her to remove her abuser's thought interruption through using the technique of *thought-stopping*. *Thought-stopping* is a method to remove unwanted thoughts. When the victim's thoughts are interrupted by the abuser coming to mind, she may dwell, obsess, or be preoccupied with thoughts that make her feel fearful, unworthy, sad, and tearful. *Thought-stopping* is encouraged to be practiced in order to change the way a victim thinks. Brain research has found that *thought-stopping* is effective. Thoughts that are connected to an emotional experience will remain in the brain's memory if the thoughts keep being repeated. She has the power to accept or reject her thoughts. As humans, we're capable of choosing what we want to consciously feel or think about. Ask her, "Which feeling do you want to think about and express?" With a new perspective, new substitute thoughts can be developed and used to replace negative, emotional thoughts that are stored in memory. This new perspective becomes her new memory.

She can either have a memorized list of positive, inspirational thoughts with which to repeatedly substitute the abuser thoughts or use a combination of other "stop" techniques recommended

RECONCILIATION ADVISOR VS. THE PROFESSIONAL

to her. But, she will not be able to develop new positive responses to her negative memories unless she develops new positive thoughts. One of my patients used to favor the technique of whispering under her breath, "delete, delete, delete" (to interrupt and stop her thoughts about the abuse or her abuser). Or shouting, if she was alone, "Transformed! Transformed! Transformed!" If the victim practices thought-stopping, the unwanted thoughts about the abuser occur less frequently. As time passes, thoughts about the abuser will be more comfortable to ignore, and at some point, they will not occur at all *unless* temporary PTSD sets in (more on treating PTSD later).

Helping the Victim Process Safety Decisions
Sometimes creating a safe environment and giving the victim a chance to save her life means requiring the victim to make major life decisions for her person. In some cases, it's not just a decision about her own person but about the other persons in her home—her children. A victim that is at the stage of prioritizing her safety and the safety of her children has become aware that as a victim, she has not been able to cope, to take care of herself, and be able to parent her children effectively. The victim, through either self-awareness or processing her lack of healthy coping skills, has come to realize that while being abused, she has not been able to respond *consistently* in appropriate ways to fulfill the needs of herself and her children.

This, in turn, has not only been to the detriment of her, but it has also negatively influenced her parental bond with her children. I have heard from children in individual and in family therapy sessions that they have anger toward their abused mother. For in their eyes, they see her as allowing the abuse to continue and keeping herself and them entrapped in it. A victim has to come to a point whereby she notices that her children need her consistent, uninterrupted nurturing more than anything, and she has to decide what she values most (their safety and bonding or the abuser).

These decisions bring on *huge* changes which involve extremely difficult, sacrificial choices that she has to make. Victims seeking safety have an epiphany that in order to restore their identity and freedom as an individual, they may have to give up everything of sentimental or material value in their life. Individual freedom for a victim comes with a great cost! Some victims of abuse may have to give up friendships, family relationships, homes, possessions, jobs, and provision for their livelihood. This is why it is so pertinent for a victim to receive the support of a professional during the process of creating safety for herself; she is losing just about everything to achieve her freedom to have an identity and to stay alive, to exist. She needs a strong alliance to uphold her quest to retrieve her pre-abuse person, to be abuse-free. She's physically alone, having left *everything* just to preserve her safety and peace of mind.

On the other hand, some victims choose not to pay the price of leaving the relationship and choose to stay as a victim. The professional must give a non-judgmental acceptance of her choice as she does have the right to self-determination. Whatever decision the victim makes, either to overcome her abuse or return to the abuse, she will always have a right to choose to stay a victim. In the same way that an abuser cannot be helped to change his abusive behaviors if he's unwilling to change, she cannot be helped if she does not want to change. A professional cannot motivate or force a victim to want to change her abusive lifestyle. The helper must respect the victim's ability to make choices for herself. Sometimes this may mean a direct conflict with what the helper believes is the right choice(s) for her circumstances. The helper can only limit the victim's right to self-determination if the victim poses a serious risk of harming herself or others.

RECONCILIATION ADVISOR VS. THE PROFESSIONAL

The professional has done his part by offering to facilitate, educate, support, and guide the victim. So long as the professional has already instilled the clear message to the victim that the abuser made a choice when he chose to hurt her and that she does not deserve to be hurt or mistreated, then the professional has done *all* that can be done at this time. The professional is now left to inform the victim that change *is* possible for her life and that the professional *will be there,* available to help whenever she decides to overcome her abuse. The message has to be that *she's not alone.*

Victims ponder seriously the question as to their readiness to give up everything. No single melodramatic or abusive episode marks the timing of the decision to take care of her safety as a victim. The transition comes gradually and naturally after a full-blown history of traumatic abuse. There is one commonality that my colleagues and I have noticed over the years in working with victims; it appears that significant decision-making takes place at that poignant time when the victim becomes aware and convinces herself to the truth—that *abuse is not love,* and therefore her abuser *does not love her.*

Once the victim makes a decision, and her choice is made for living a permanent, safe life without abuse, *nothing temporary matters.* The victim is *now* officially ready to make the changes she wants to make in her life. It is at this point that the victim obtains the empowerment of predictability in her life; she discovers that she can indeed count on her own self, and even begins (through gaining trust in a therapeutic alliance) to meet other people that she can begin to count on for her safety. Granted, she will now be more observant and evaluative of trust factors than before her abuse, and she may be more careful than usual about being vulnerable to intimacy, but she will have at least ventured out of her abused, isolated state. Learning to establish safety teaches the victim to build her own confidence in knowing *how* to protect herself.

Role Modeling a Balance of Trust & Self-Protection
When it comes to safety with others, the victim now has to re-learn the balance between being appropriately trusting and self-protective. Through her professional relationship with her therapist, she learns to connect with another person while at the same time preserving her autonomy that she has regained. The victim's learning how to stay safe and how to take good care of her own self is a euphoric *eureka* experience! She now unquestionably understands that she deserves a well-lived life. If she has children and she decides to protect herself along with her children, they begin to gradually regain their trust in her capacity to nurture them. If the abuser continues to indirectly abuse her through the children (as is discussed in this book), the ability to maintain a nurturing bond with them and restore their reciprocation continues to be a challenge that requires additional therapeutic work.

Developing a Safety Escape Plan (SEP) with a victim in the initial stages of treatment can become quite taxing with some cases because the therapeutic trust alliance has not yet been established. This, in turn, places the professional in the responsibility of initiating an active role with a frightened victim. Typically, a victim of abuse scans her territory cautiously before taking any initiative, almost expecting some form of retaliation from others (including the therapist) for acting on her own behalf. Normal human tendency is to be comfortable with trial and error, but for a victim of abuse, her common sense for using initiative has been ill-treated (and for some, destroyed). This restricts her capacity to take risks to help herself or to ask for help for fear of punishment from her abuser, now expecting the therapist to do the same.

RECONCILIATION ADVISOR VS. THE PROFESSIONAL

Here is a word of caution on biases during a victim assessment on behalf of the helper. As the research shows, abuse does not discriminate; in fact, discrimination and prejudices usually only come into play from the abuser and when the helper is evaluating. A review of the evaluator's discriminatory factors and the victim's profile are important as part of the assessment process. The helper and the victim come into the relationship with their own perception backgrounds based on their training, attitude, partiality, and assumptions about abuse. A victim comes in with her own context of her abuse, and what she's experiencing reveals her discriminatory factors regarding abuse (victim's fear, isolation level, perception, and knowledge on all forms of abuse; her past and present influences from people/community/world norms; her awareness of access to resources; her decreased sense of self; her lack of clarity about healthy standards of behavior and of what normal degrees of power and life satisfaction are). There are a host of discriminatory factors which contribute to the helper-victim relationship process. These factors will identify the level of both the professional's and the victim's own discrimination toward abuse.

In order to provide objective, self-aware, patient-centered treatment, it's most useful to eliminate the presence of discrimination barriers on behalf of the helper and the victim. It is the helper's responsibility to access his own personal discrimination about abuse. The most effective way that helpers can assist a victim is by assessing and being aware of their own biases toward abuse, and, in conjunction, to do a thorough intake on the victim's discriminatory factors toward abuse. The number of significant factors to consider in assessing the victim's abuse-discrimination levels include, but are not limited to, the following: anxiety and depression levels, beliefs about victim myths (such as that she provokes his abuse, that her abuse is a private matter, or that it's the drugs and alcohol that cause the abuse or his unresolved anger/stress/depression), normalizing abuse due to frequent past direct/indirect exposure to abuse, limited knowledge about the dynamics of abuse, a lack of understanding of the legal process and her rights, unawareness of or consciously strained relationships with community resource providers, or restricted access to those resources that are available to her.

Some victims of abuse are consciously passive to protect themselves on the outside, but on the inside, they are anything but passive. They sit quietly brewing for weeks, months, or years; like a heated, boiling volcano ready to erupt, they are anything but helpless. Victims are programmed by their abusers that there is no room for common error; a victim has been *brainwashed* to believe that being independent of the abuser's control renders her as disobedient and an unacceptable wife. With a victim, the professional's sensitive initiative in the initial sessions is sometimes needed for the process of voicing her pain and reconstructing her life to begin. The professional has to delicately balance the victim's right to self-determination with protecting her safety and her children's safety. The professional is faced with the challenge of listening and asking therapeutic questions that will help the victim identify the reasons for her current symptoms and the implications in light of her current and past circumstances. This approach prevents her from sitting in her silence, ready to explode. This initiative on behalf of the professional not only allows the victim to break her silence appropriately, but it also allows for the professional to come closer to stepping into her world of darkness and providing safety.

Choice words for the professional are of calculated importance at all times, but they are even more important while working with an abused victim. Victims of abuse come from a severed relationship that has damaged *most*, if not all, of her significant relationships. It is within your role as a professional to model and guide the traumatized victim into appropriate

RECONCILIATION ADVISOR VS. THE PROFESSIONAL

relational interaction. Professionals have the privilege of guiding the healthy relationship bonding that first develops through the therapeutic relationship between the professional and the victim and then extends into the victim's significant relationships. The professional relationship can impact the outcome of the victim electing to empower herself from a victim to an *Overcomer*. The professional's social support of the victim can alleviate the victim's symptoms, while a neutral stance may stimulate a resurgence of her symptoms. A victim of spousal abuse is extremely vulnerable; her sense of self has been destroyed and can only be restored gradually, as it originated—by trusting and bonding with others.

The emotional bonding that victims of abuse pursue from family and friends varies in the levels of intimacy that they desire; it vacillates and changes during the treatment phases. Naturally, at the beginning phase of treatment when the crisis of the abuse is still at the escalated stage, the primary intervention is to develop the trust that will be the foundation to the resolution of the abuse. An oath of *confidentiality* to the victim and the commitment to her *protection* and *safety* is pivotal and is a matter of life and death importance. This is important because in normal relationships, the person does not expect to be betrayed, but as a victim, she knows all too well that she is fragile and has been denounced and has repeatedly experienced breach of trust.

A professional has to be explicit about his intentions for treatment with a victim that appears flustered and paranoid about potential harm being done to her. Sometimes working with a victim means receiving an oppositional, uncooperative attitude from her; remember that she's acting this way out of fear and defensiveness. Don't even *think about* how this is a thankless job! Instead, remind yourself that she's a deeply hurt, traumatized woman. Ignore her instigative intimidation tactic if her attitude expresses that she can work all this out on her own and then proceeds to share all of her accolades (including the psychology courses she has taken). Besides, you're just a patsy, so you better watch out! She might go the extra mile and threaten to report you to the authorities/her attorney/your licensure for invading her/her family's privacy; even if you're a mandated reporter and she's the one who sought you out for assistance with her abuse.

It's so crucial not to personalize her opposition to accepting any help and to remember that victims of trauma have a mindless intentionality of hurting others because for the most part, they are on an offensive autopilot before they heal. By focusing on offering victim treatment options and setting boundaries, there's a potential hope that if the victim accepts a reparative experience for her treatment plan, her brain limbic system (responsible for memories, mood, emotions, motivation, instinct, nurturing) with time can be rewired and thereby reduce the biochemistry of her traumatic stress.

In order to create an *Overcomer*, de-stressed, emotional climate that will be conducive to an abuse-free lifestyle, repeated positive therapeutic experiences will be necessary. While in session, the victim must mourn losses and engage in role-playing (*Overcomer* rehearsals) so as to challenge or replace her chronic denial and victim unproductive cognitive thought patterns. Intermittent assurances are necessary with some victims for whom the initial verbal commitment to provide ethical, safe support is not enough. Through the treatment interventions which focus on the unacceptable maltreatment she has experienced, her derailment in accepting her victimization can transfer into beginning to accept and reciprocate care and nurture; she even catches up on receiving affection/love from others. At some point, she develops these processes which were stymied by her trauma. Over time, the victim is able to relearn healthy comfort levels regarding her need for closeness and distance in relationships. It is as if she goes through the process of separation-individuation from her first years of life bonding, and eventually she is able to reestablish that autonomy now as an *Overcomer*. The treatment goal is to, step by step, therapeutically regulate the balance of love, intimacy, and aggression to a healthy level.

The act of positive relationship-building works in more than one way; it reinstates the victim's sense *and* view of self along with regenerating her self-respect. However, this self-respect is a therapeutic accomplishment that is steadily gained. It's acquired throughout the work that she does on dealing with what was done to her and *what* she had to do in order to survive. Her past compromising of her values and loss of morality periodically visit her both during sessions and on her own. The professional has to assist her with this struggle so that she can put it to rest. A professional has to provide reality-based therapy in reiterating to her that her past actions are not her fault and that *it is* her abusive spouse that has committed the crimes against her.

Providing Support When the Victim Regresses
The victim will at times throughout the process of leaving her victim role experience faltering steps. This can either be a temporary loss of momentum as she works toward becoming an *Overcomer*, or it can mean that she's not quite at a developmental phase where she can completely work on restoring her sense of self. Be patient with her and just delicately provide the tools once again. Help her to realize that it takes time to unlearn old negative messages and behaviors but that even if the healing is gradual, it will come! It's helpful to remember that a victim will experience cognitive dissonance (anxiety from double-minded thoughts about the abuser when she feels fondness for him but anger and hurt toward his abusiveness at the same time). In a victim-trauma mind, early recovery symptoms can include missing the abuser because of the cognitive dissonance that reflects

back on the loving, good times and the blurring or veiling of objective reality. As long as safety has been established and unwavering hope is provided, the victim's pace determines how she works on each goal that she has set for herself.

What the victim has done to save her life is common to all attempting to survive crimes against them. She has to renounce her guilt, shame, and unforgiving spirit toward herself and others through the professional's and others' fair assessments of her conduct in the present. She needs to renew her own value. She has been living a dishonest, abnormal life by being a victim and doing whatever the abuser required of her behind closed doors while being a normal person in front of others. Realistic assessments from the professional dissolve her feelings of humiliation and self-condemnation. This is a critical phase of treatment; *any careless words* can ignite the victim's self-blame and aggravate the victim's progress in restoring her self-respect. It's useful to validate the psychological damage that the abuser has done with her morality while at the same time restating that with her effort, this harm can also be undone. It's important to anonymously reinforce examples of other victims that have been in similar abusive circumstances and illustrate the universal dilemma that faces those entrapped in abusive relationships: acknowledging the extremely limited choices in moral judgment which *all* victims experience.

Sometimes it is because of a lack of forgiveness that progress in treatment is at a plateau or regressive state. This is because forgiveness redefines oneself and those others in the past and in the present by replacing self-defense or protective mechanisms, feelings of anger, resentment, bitterness, grudges, anxiety, fear, and anguish toward self and others with compassion and empathy. The victim may not be able to currently or ever understand "why" others have hurt her, but simply learning to adjust cognitive and spiritual thought processes will follow the

RECONCILIATION ADVISOR VS. THE PROFESSIONAL

act of forgiveness, which will then produce self- and others' acceptance (in spite of the trauma they have caused). Forgiveness can only occur when negative cognitive and spiritual thought patterns no longer control the victim; this is a critical step in the healing of a victim who then becomes an *Overcomer*. For the victim to aspire to become an *Overcomer*, the helper must convey hope and a belief in her strengths and competencies and teach her the *Overcomer* skills that foster mastery in living free from abuse.

It's not always a smooth road with a victim of abuse as she becomes educated about her victimization. The road can become bumpy because learning about her condition may *increase* her *vulnerability* because this learning focuses on areas that *increase* her awareness of her unhappiness and risk of harm's way. She has also been pre-conditioned to make others happy or make others love her; it's difficult for her to accept positive feedback and validation at face value without having to do something for it. Victims may undervalue the professional's therapeutic intervention because they're not used to being respected or receiving positive personal recognition. Many victims experience discomfort and have difficulty *accepting* caring, personal regard. The *key* is to *notice* and *reinforce* every small step that she initiates and takes toward self-improvement.

Remember that the abuser will go through all extremes, even when not physically in front of her, to penetrate her mind and to re-hook her back into his realm of crazy. Or, the abuser may make contact during the victim's vulnerable *Overcomer* recovery stage and pretend to have changed, asking for a trial reassurance of his changed ways by "just being friends" and, if there are children, "staying together for their sake," speaking as if this has been a healthy, natural end of their relationship. She needs a refresher that this was not a normal, average end of their relationship; that it is not a typical love relationship that has been through an ordinary breakup; that it is the termination of an abusive relationship with an abnormal person; that his attempt to sway the victim is just more of the abuser's romantic, flirtatious tomfoolery; and that returning to him is just taking the chance of being bamboozled again.

For an outcome of *Overcomer* success, the helper must remain calm, positive, and communicative of the expectation of success (in spite of the helper's awareness that the victim may at times speak hopelessly, negatively, become frustrated or overwhelmed, and think it is impossible to be free from her past abuse and/or her abuser). It is during the relapse pitfall times that the helper must bring back to the victim's unwary mind the importance of maintaining her focus and encourage her to draw from her spiritual strength and from her *Overcomer* principles. Working with a victim of abuse requires the helper to be flexible and adaptive. The victim has to re-learn trust and may remain visually and emotionally labile in the beginning, middle, or later stages of interacting with the helper. Due to the victim's past controlled life, the helper must not be rigid and should have a willingness to be spontaneous in knowing when to be gentle (but direct), non-directive, respect or redirect defenses, confront or support choices, revisit past trauma, or focus on the here-and-now or future. Without a balanced helper and victim involvement whereby a reciprocal relationship exists in that the helper and the victim have the same outcome goal (the victim wants a lifetime capacity to eliminate an abusive dysfunctional life), *Overcomer* success is limited. Both the helper and the victim *must* be patient, remain calm, and be goal-oriented.

How does a victim helper remain calm, not get frustrated with victim relapses, and remain flexible for the victim to choose overcoming her abuse? By assisting the victim to recognize (bring to mind) that which is not helpful to her abuse-free goals. Identify and challenge her ineffective victim mentality

RECONCILIATION ADVISOR VS. THE PROFESSIONAL

beliefs, attitudes, and behaviors. Challenging the victim is not an aggressive approach; it is actually bringing her back to the reality of sound thinking and intervening on her current victim-like thoughts and actions, which is not going to fly in the reality of her goals. Non-reality-based thinking impedes the victim's clear thinking. Offer supportive, clear suggestions, alternatives, skills, instruction, time-sensitive (yet therapeutic) homework assignments, and direction through a non-condemning, non-judgmental, non-shaming approach. Use successive approximation in your efforts to promote change (one step/strategy at a time, followed by validation of positive change). Gradually building up on successes assists the victim in shifting from a self-recrimination or self-induced shame/guilt perspective to an appropriate conviction to desire healthy changes for herself; in turn, this further develops her self-esteem, emotional IQ, responsibility to self and others, and moral character. Success will be accomplished as you, the helper, provide or suggest a non-threatening environment where she can be free to role-play, rehearse, and engage in newfound activities, and practice, practice, practice her new *Overcomer* ways!

As the victim leaves her regressive state and progresses from her *survival mode* into an *Overcomer* role, she learns to release from her grip those aspects of herself that were formed by her abuse; she becomes more forgiving of herself. She has given up her sense of *false hope* for reconciliation into a healthy marriage with the abuser. She has grieved the loss of the abusive relationship that she has had to accept could never become a harmonious relationship. She has learned that it only takes one person to forgive and two for reconciliation. She has forgiven her abuser by realizing that she doesn't have to depend on his non-trustworthy apologies in order to forgive him and move on with her life. She has found that it is preferably peaceful not to carry the load of anger and an unforgiving heart toward her abuser.

She has gained insight into the religious guilt-trip from her abuser or others of having to stay in her abusive relationship because she is expected to forgive seventy times seven. She has come to realize that although he was supposed to be her intimate friend that she could trust, he is far from trustworthy in her relationship with him. She now knows that an intimate relationship is based on trust and maintained through respect for the others' confidentiality. However, when the abuser's entitled need *insists* on telling *all* that the victim has shared with him about her personal agenda or life to whomever he can, the victim's trust continues to be betrayed; she then remains a victim of his apologies, violations of privacy, and his arrogant exploitation of her behind her back or in the presence of others, and that is not acceptable.

The prospective *Overcomer* is no longer willing to live in the betrayal trap as a victim of abuse; she refuses to stay and to continue to live in this trap, using her maladaptive coping skills. Instead, she has learned healthy coping skills with which to live her life. While emotional and/or physical violence was once a way of life for her, her life has now become a *safe haven*, and she has become grateful for no longer having to live in an *atmosphere of terror*. As a potential *Overcomer*, she is now able to acknowledge how her character was affected by the abuse because she has now learned that the damage does not have to live with her permanently. The more that a victim is willing to extrapolate from her past abuse, the more she's capable of accepting the memory of herself having been abused. It is at this point that she will work jointly with the therapist to create her *Overcomer* therapeutic goals and work toward rebuilding her life.

Cognitive Behavioral Therapy (CBT) & Reality Therapy (RT)
As a therapist, I have found *Cognitive Behavioral Therapy* (CBT) *and Reality Therapy* (RT) highly effective when working with victims of abuse. CBT was founded by a psychiatrist, Aaron T. Beck

M.D., in the 1960s. It was further developed in the 1970s and has been implemented successfully with patients for the decades since then. CBT is a therapeutic method that helps to identify and rectify specific errors in one's thinking. Distorted, erroneous thoughts (cognitive distortions) produce negative thoughts or painful feelings which influence a person's maladaptive reactions, ways of thinking, and decision-making skills, resulting in poor judgment and unproductive behavioral choices. CBT was developed as a treatment approach in an effort to modify a person's thought patterns, alter emotional states, and improve management skills of the self by intervening on the factors that contribute to the onset or continuation of mentally unbalanced behaviors, including anxiety and depression. CBT is a treatment of choice because it is when a person is experiencing distressful thoughts that the most effective point of intervention can occur.

CBT can have both an outcome of short- and long-term benefits for the victim. CBT, when properly applied, aids the person's mindset in thinking healthier thoughts and making better choices. If changes are made in thinking (distorted thoughts), changes in emotions and behavior follow (preventing self-defeating behaviors). Research indicates that cognitive therapy reduces the rate of regression into maladaptive behaviors. CBT strategies and techniques are always employed at the person's pace of growth, yet they deliver visible relief of symptoms early on. CBT works well with victims because it intervenes on the faulty thinking and cognitive distortions with which a victim enters therapy. CBT focuses on helping the victim understand how her negative or distorted thinking causes or contributes to her victim role. The goal of CBT is to help the victim identify and change her faulty thinking on her own in order to internally feel better about her choices and, in turn, experience more positive behaviors, even when her external circumstances remain the same. Strategic CBT interventions are applied to complete the treatment goals and enhance treatment outcome (safety and giving up the victim role). Working from the start on correcting the faulty thoughts implanted by the abuser that she has learned to own will intercept those thoughts (abuser's beliefs, false self-beliefs), which can improve her mood and dim outlook.

Once a trusting, therapeutic alliance has been established with the victim, the therapy sessions are to be structured in such a way that the victim allows the therapist (without projecting that he is attempting to control her) the liberty to challenge her whenever she digresses into maladaptive thinking and behaviors. The idea is to break her pattern of maladaptive *reactive* thinking and behaving to learn to practice healthy *responding*, which is a more adaptive way of coping. The goal through CBT is to replace her past negative cognitions, emotions, and behaviors with positive coping skills.

Reality Therapy (RT) was founded by psychiatrist William Glasser, M.D., in the 1960s. It is a beneficial therapy when working with victims because it does not focus on mental diagnosis; RT concentrates on the three Rs: realism, responsibility, and right-and-wrong. RT approaches the victim with the realism of her circumstances, responsibilities at hand, and using discernment in right and wrong. Glasser posits that when humans are unable to attain their basic needs, their behavior breaks away from the norm, resulting in personal and social problems. Therefore, RT is used as a tool to develop the victim's ability to problem-solve in order to create a better present and future for her and her children. The victim is encouraged to seek becoming more actively aware of what she *really* needs and wants, how she is behaving, and what choices she is currently making in order to make choices that will best achieve her behavioral goals for her life. (RT *is* a Choice Theory, more on this later).

Reality Therapy is ideal in treating the victim because it stops the abuser's censorship on her right to feel and it gives her the freedom to disclose her feelings which have been ignored or unpermitted; she no longer has to turn her back on her emotions, which equals to denial of reality. Speaking and listening to her feelings gives her wounded heart a voice. It is this candor with her emotions that ushers her into the reality of her past and present circumstances; it proposes a vision for her future. She learns that change can only come through her vulnerable, honest processing of her thoughts and feelings. Reality Therapy gives her permission to emotionally feel and to have healthy interaction with herself and others around her. Reality Therapy provides an experiential affirmation which brings the victim back to her existence and identity of who she truly is and is meant to be.

CBT can be combined with RT to assist the victim in becoming aware of her tendency to think negatively, as she has been drilled to do, and learn to replace the grimness with positive thoughts that are more of a *reality*. RT approaches the victim with the realism of her circumstances, responsibilities at hand, and using discernment in right and wrong. While it's important for the victim to ventilate her past abuse, it is equally important to treat the present and what can be resolved in the here-and-now; this helps to simultaneously alleviate her symptoms and her recurrent vulnerable state. CBT and RT are effective with victims in both individual and group therapy; they are therapeutic interventions that she can take with her and use as self-help skills.

Therapeutic homework assignments are useful in developing the victim's ability to use CBT and RT on her own. When a victim completes homework assignments, it empowers her as well as fulfills her commitment to make permanent choices and changes in her life in the presence or absence of her therapist. CBT and RT serve victims best because they are therapies that require the complete involvement of the patient; they empower her to be in control of her life with the therapist listening and modeling patience without being authoritarian and simply being her guide.

A Family Systems Approach to Restoration of Identity
Victims of abuse generally suffer from the loss of their personal identity through the abuser. Sometimes victims also suffer through being abandoned/disowned by family members or by having to establish no contact with toxic family members. On the upside, those relationships she has lost can serve as a positive aspect of healing from the problem of losing her identity through the victim becoming knowledgeable about her background in family and interpersonal relating. Strong, supportive relationships, not necessarily blood-related, can be included in identifying those that influence her environment and affect her functioning. A victim can purposely decide to grow into her own true separate self-identity by *differentiating* herself from her family upbringing, and others' negative influence. It was Murray Bowen, a psychiatrist and professor of psychiatry who developed a Family Systems Model and coined the term *differentiation*.

Differentiation refers to a person's ability to identify their own personal goals and values apart from the mental coercion of those around them. A Family Systems and *differentiation* approach can be used in order for the victim not to make decisions just based on feelings but instead to learn to think clearly, carefully, and in a solid way when making choices. Family Systems focuses on family and significant others' relationships as a key factor in a person's mental health. Family Systems promotes the nurturing and development of the positive relationships that do exist within the family or support system in comparison to those relationships that only bring negative influences or the risk of identity theft.

A victim who learns to *differentiate* herself from her abuser and other significant relationships is able to maintain her convictions, own her beliefs, and set her own direction for a healthy life regardless of the pressures from the control of others' approval or disapproval. She is able to be herself without needing their affirmations or validation because she recognizes that they don't have a clear sense of who they are, and she does. She no longer has to depend on their identity to have self-worth and a sense of self.

Dr. Murray Bowen's Family Systems Model teaches that it's expected family members, peers, colleagues, friends or others in a relationship with the newly *differentiated* person may oppose the choice to *differentiate* and that there are generally three stages of opposition that take place: Stage One, you're told that you're wrong for changing and the reasons why; Stage Two, you're asked to change back, and you will be accepted again; and Stage Three, you're warned that if you don't change back to your old self there will be consequences which are listed for you. The Family Systems approach is applied to promote healthy functioning within the family or support system by each member standing firm on their principles in spite of opposition from members that want to derail that person's clear, solid thinking (mindfulness).

A victim that restores her identity through a *differentiation* of herself apart from her dysfunctional relationships is prepared that her abuser and other *undifferentiated* people in her life will oppose when she matures in her level of *differentiation*. But this is no different than the powerful opposition that a victim faces when she leaves her abuser, or when she accepts Christ as her Savior and source of identity. *Differentiation* will challenge the deeply mal-ingrained, multigenerational, dysfunctional behavioral patterns in her family or other relationships.

Family Systems aids the victim in her journey to becoming an *Overcomer*. It is a useful strategy in restoring her identity because it emphasizes how change can take place in her life and benefit her as a result of knowing her family history and how others' interactions impact her life. A tool that Dr. Murray Bowen invented and used in Family Systems intervention is the genogram; it is recommended to be used as a part of the victim researching and processing her family and other close relationships. A genogram assists in the explaining of a person's family and relationship dynamics. The genogram is a pictorial diagram drawn of a person's family and other emotionally bonded relationship attachments: in order to recognize and depict an image of the medical and mental health, hereditary patterns and data that are marked with repetitive behaviors and tendencies to inherit. A person does not have to live with someone or have had contact with a previous generation to inherit their spiritual, emotional, or physical behaviors.

The use of a genogram for a victim is a valuable resource because it provides a basis for her to discover some of the destructive behavioral patterns that she may be unaware are linked to her maladaptive, dysfunctional behaviors that were first manifested within her family or other relationships A genogram allows the victim to hold on to the identity of who she *is* and who she is *not* or *does not* want to become. The genogram can assist a victim in better knowing herself and her relationships; it can be used to create precautionary and preventive measures to *differentiate* her person and maintain her own personal identity that supports her goals, morals, and principles in her life. A victim and her therapist can use a Family Systems approach and make good use of a genogram to assess the positive and negative family and relationship attachments and decide where intervention may be most helpful to reduce and curtail family and relationship abusive dysfunction. Generally, genograms are hand-drawn and sketched while processing in therapy, but if a victim prefers or is unable to establish a therapeutic relationship and has access to a computer, there is genogram commercial software on the internet, or, using a tablet, she can create her own genogram on iGenogram.

A Neurological Approach to Victim Trauma

Professionals recognize the valuable benefits and the optimism involved in using CBT due to its neurological workings of the brain. Daniel Siegel, M.D., Richard Davidson, PhD, and others have done substantial research with extensive accounts; they have reported predictions which have produced empirical confirmations that our interpersonal relationships and neural systems form our mind (brain) throughout our lifespan. This exhaustive, thorough work of neuroscientists, developmental psychologists, and clinicians has been able to document research on subjects and verify supportive evidence of how the mind, body, and relationships interplay to make connections in the brain. From the very beginning of the therapeutic relationship, the professional is already intervening on the victim's brain development by connecting with the victim's emotions *before* redirecting her behavior.

An experienced professional knows to initially connect with the victim's right brain's nonverbal attributes. All of the right brain empathic gestures, facial expressions, listening and pausing, and the providing of comfort with a relationship safety net for the victim in a calm tone of voice invite the victim to allow the therapist at some point to redirect her to her left brain for effective processing. Once the victim's right brain establishes trust in the professional, the professional can then redirect her left brain to express in words (as she hears his gentle words of communication) the logical explanations for her victimization. Now that the left brain is more actively working with the right brain, solutions can be presented, and planning can take place along with the setting of new boundaries. Thus, the victim can learn about left and right brain interactions within the context of relational experiences through this cognitive therapy.

Many victims are surprised to learn that *all* of our relational experiences are neurological. Training the victim about the brain doesn't have to turn into lengthy neuroscientific sessions. It can be as basic as teaching about *brain integration* and reflecting on the fact that relational experiences give us brain clues as to what to expect (left or right brain experience with another). A victim should learn that gaining insight into whether to expect an emotional desert or an emotional volcano when interacting with someone is an advantage for her health and that of others' well-being. She should be informed that the healthiest strategy is to intentionally force the left and the right brain to work together. Suggesting to the victim to practice use of both the left and right brain in processing and in her interactions may at first be grueling for her, but ultimately, she will experience and reap the rewards of the harmony that right-and left-brain integration bring. Ultimately, through brain integration, the victim will be able to regulate her thinking and behavior. This outcome is achieved through the process of her working with the professional's assistance, so in essence, it becomes a work of co-regulation. It is imperative for the professional to also consistently regulate his left and right brain approaches in her treatment.

A professional's compassion for the victim, maintaining the patient's right to self-determination, and ethical responsibility to the victim runs parallel to the success of the therapeutic goals set for treatment. As has been discussed previously, a victim usually presents herself with overwhelming thoughts and feelings prior to treatment. It stands to reason that a professional can work with her to create her treatment goals but that she has to be continually reassured that there are short-term and long-term goals; in most instances, it's one goal at a time, and generally all goals overlap one another to eventually complete the treatment outcomes.

A professional can only work with a victim at the level that she is willing to employ the treatment goals for her life. Some victims are not ready to make any permanent changes in their abusive life and are not open to setting neurological treatment goals for themselves and their children. Regardless, the professional's understanding must always be readily available and unbiased. Just like the victim can't change the abuser, the professional can't change the victim. It is the victim's responsibility to strategize her goals for change with the professional; at the same time, it is the professional's ethical responsibility to educate and guide her solely with the therapeutic tools that can help her to achieve what she has set out to accomplish for herself.

The Middle Prefrontal Cortex (MPFC) of the brain has the duty to plan complex, cognitive behavior; it takes charge of decision-making, expresses the self, and regulates behavior. It is remarkably important to develop the MPFC when working with a victim of abuse trauma. The MPFC regulates social control so one does not experience socially unacceptable results. Neurological *self-regulation* of the mind and body is in the interest of the victim if she is to overcome her abuse. *Self-regulation* is defined as her ability to begin to think about her thought processes and to take responsibility for evaluating and controlling those thoughts and her behaviors. This further entails her willingness to monitor those thoughts and actions and her progress against the goals that she has established for herself and her children. Self-regulation requires the victim's motivation to learn new ways of thinking and interacting with the self and others. The victim's benefit in choosing to self-regulate is that it provides her with the autonomy to monitor her self-improvement goals.

Neurological self-regulation gives the victim a new set of skills whereby she can become cognizant of her day-to-day experiences and appropriately check if her activities correspond to her goals and to change her strategies as necessary; for it is *all* within her own control to troubleshoot whenever she regresses to her dysfunctional ways of thinking and relating. Self-regulation allows the victim to monitor and evaluate daily if her thoughts and actions are running side-by-side with her ultimate (long-term) desired outcome. A victim self-regulates by empowering herself to control her emotions and habits. Anxiety and the amygdala are so powerful that victims report the symptoms include that their eyesight is affected while under high anxiety with haziness and an inability to see clearly, even when they are wearing their eyeglasses. Neurologically, a therapist can assist the victim with anxiety-based symptoms, including PTSD, by teaching her how to work with strengthening the use of her MPFC and balancing her amygdala, which then rewires her brain into a healthier, relaxed state.

The contrast of developing the MPFC is to have the victim remain under the operation of the amygdala, which is responsible for activating her emotional states (repetitive responses, intense and impulsive reactions, sometimes obsessive-compulsive behaviors). Like with all parts of the brain, each part is absolutely necessary to play its role. However, when the victim primarily functions out of the amygdala, she's at risk for acting before thinking; it's as if she's robbed of her ability to use calm, logical thinking. Walter Bradford Cannon taught us and warned us about our amygdala's fight-or-flight-or-freeze response. Typically, a hyperarousal state of flight or freeze is the response for the victim who operates under the amygdala's dominance.

The therapeutic process can help her learn that functioning through only one part of her brain when undergoing stressful events or managing relationships only serves to hijack her prefrontal cortex (reasoning capacity). She can learn that this only sets herself up to operate under the emergency operation of the amygdala (fight, flight, freeze mode). The amygdala is an extremely important part of our brain, but if used alone, it tends to do its job—alerting us of threats to our survival. This means that if the victim operates solely under the direction of the amygdala, the victim will tend to receive daily living stressors as if there is a dangerous survival risk.

A victim's sole use of her amygdala will result in extreme fear and anxiety on her behalf, implementing coping mechanisms that only invite a flight or freeze mode (no problem-solving fight coping mechanisms). In order for a victim to move from the amygdala reactive position into an *Overcomer* (responsive) position, she has to intentionally become self-aware and quickly alert and orientate herself times four into a brain integration, appropriate, assertive fight mode. Notice the key working word is *appropriate*; whereas, the inappropriate fight mode is out of control, nonproductive, aggressive behavior. A victim succeeds in becoming an *Overcomer* because she finally becomes her own entity and asserts herself, as opposed to not having self-awareness and lacking a sense of self; this she accomplishes through directing and regulating her own thoughts, actions, and relationships. Further, she's now equipped to teach and pass on self-regulation to others, preventing the next generation from an inability to regulate the self.

The CBT treatment goals for a victim to gain brain integration should include working to allow the victim to confront her fears, to regulate her emotions, to be able to tell her story, to seek sound decision-making through thinking before acting, to consider the consequences of her choices, to refrain from impulsive choices, to practice rational problem-solving, to learn to adjust and adapt her own and others' communication, to process and consider moral issues, to define clear boundaries, and to develop empathy for others. Such treatment goals will allow her to self-regulate her thoughts and behaviors. The end result is body regulation, emotional balance, fear modulation, response flexibility, attuned communication, empathy, self-insight, morality with intuition, and the ability to plan and execute her plans. Since this is a co-regulation therapeutic relationship, the professional has to continuously think *intentionally* about checking which approach (left or right brain) is not balanced in his interventions.

CBT requires the victim to be engaged in the therapeutic process; using the wrong brain approach can further enrage the victim. In other words, professionals are responsible for reflecting and evaluating their own functioning and uses of the left and right brain—checking for their own personal, balanced integration. Unbalanced *brain integration* leads to rarely using the right or left brain together, which brings disharmony in processing and social interactions (dysregulation) for both the victim and the professional.

The professional's comprehension of the specific parts of the brain that need to be developed in treating the victim is preeminent. For instance, the Middle Prefrontal Cortex (MPFC), if highly developed, can lead to an excellent prognosis for the victim. Developing her MPFC helps her to achieve self-regulation of her thoughts and behaviors. This is because the MPFC is responsible for so many areas of self-regulation. A well-developed MPFC can aid her in developing personal intuition and insight about herself and others, unlearning rigidity and gaining flexibility, regulating her emotions with balance while unlearning anxiousness and fear, adjusting and adapting communication with self and others, discernment with morals, and learning empathy for others. Such self-regulation affects her *entire* autonomic nervous system, which is responsible for regulating her heart rate, breathing, and other body functions.

Once the victim's MPFC is developing, she can now make *mindfully-aware,* sound decisions and choices as to whether to take a different direction or intentionally take the same path.

When the MPFC is tuned in, the mind now knows and has the ability to intentionally change its course for a greater purpose. The victim now has the flexibility to reflect on the past cognitively and allow her life to unfold functionally by focusing only on using her past as a valued experience that has taught her insightful growth for the present and future. When the victim's left-brain functioning is increasing in use and she is telling her story coherently, it is an opportune time to encourage her to process her family system relational attachments (covering her family of origin, other caretakers, and immediate family).

It is beneficial for her treatment outcomes to get in touch with what type of familial attachments she has experienced and to be educated on the differences (secure attachment or suboptimal attachment). Parental and/or caretaker attachments impact neurological development from birth and throughout the lifespan. A secure attachment means she formed a healthy, strong emotional bond with her parents and/or caregivers, which fortified a positive social/emotional development. A suboptimal attachment means she received insecure forms of attachment whereby her parents and/or caretakers were inconsistent in their availability, care, or presence thereby disrupting or severing the parent/caretaker bond. If the victim is uncertain about the history of her attachment in primary relationships, there are free attachment style tests online which she can take to help her discern and understand the dynamics of her attachment background.

Attachment & Brain Dominance
The time she spends on drawing a narrative of her parent-child attachment recollections is also a good time to decipher the type of parent-child attachment that she's currently practicing at home with her children. Much of her work on identifying her parental attachment history and the history she has thus far created with her own children involves becoming willing in her fragility to

recollect her past parental messages. This process also helps to bring to her awareness any experiences growing up whereby she observed or felt an inability to make decisions, double-standard gender roles, impulsive behaviors, out-of-control anger, fear of being rejected, unexplained need to be in power or gain control of others, and exploiting boundaries.

Once she has allowed herself to become vulnerable to retrieving her past parental messages and experiences, she can then begin to make reasonable connections between the parental messages she received and her proceeding life experiences. For example, if she recalls persistent patterns of being called offensive names, being referred to in insulting terms, or receiving messages such as, "No matter what you say or do, it's not going to amount to a hill of beans" or "you *cannot do that* because *I* said so," those messages would be coming from suboptimal parenting. It's important to note that not all messages and experiences in childhood are sent by parents; strong messages can also take root from significant others that are the primary caretakers when the parents are at work.

In blended families, the children may experience secure parental messages in one parental home, and during visitations, they may receive suboptimal messages from the other parent overtly or covertly. The professional's role at this time is to simply be *present* for the victim when she begins to make connections as to how the early childhood messages have conditioned her to respond or react to her current relationships. Identifying childhood and even present parental messages can be useful in connecting to the messages she currently gives to herself, her children, and others. If a victim has experienced or is currently experiencing suboptimal parental attachment messages, the message from the professional to the victim has to be, "You do not have to be whatever the negative messages say that you are." She can learn to dominate her own brain and the way she thinks.

RECONCILIATION ADVISOR VS. THE PROFESSIONAL

It is not only a decision-making time to resolve her childhood and present parent-child attachment experiences as an adult with her own parents, but it's also a decision time for the type of parental attachment that she would like to choose to have with her own children. Once educated on parental attachment, it is never too late to start to re-parent her own self by making amends (forgiving suboptimal parental experiences), and it's certainly never undue or overdue to re-parent her own children with a secure parental attachment. She will need some positive strokes from the professional to commend her on her decision to interact with her family of origin *and* immediate family using whole-brain integration, choosing to provide a secure attachment!

If a victim is operating from the MPFC at the initial stages of therapy, although she may be *acting* manipulative and controlling of the therapeutic recommendations, she can ultimately be reasoned with to make sound decisions for the safety of herself and her children; she can learn that she's still in control of her life (even if she follows the therapist's recommendations to regulate her behavior). A professional's response to a victim's difficult, authentically-reactive left brain with a "won't do it" attitude is not to return difficult for difficult. If she's functioning at that high level of left-brain reactivity and the defensive "I won't follow recommendations" attitude persists, the upside of that type of response is that the victim *does want* some control of her own life. The professional's response is to emphasize authority (recommendations) while also balancing the delivery of the instructions with warmth. The goal is to elevate her thinking—to deescalate her and not escalate her.

Some victims present themselves in right brain "can't do it" attitudes in total distress. They feel and act as if they have (and indeed, they have) lost complete control of their lives. Stress hormones have overtaken the victim, and she feels as if she can't reason what has happened to her in her relationship with the abuser. The victim feels that she *can't* make decisions and choices. At this state of distress, it's not only that she finds herself unable to concentrate and reason, but she can also be difficult to process and reason with—unless the professional is willing and able to respond with warmth and comfort wrapped with authority on the recommendations. It is to the professional's advantage in meeting treatment goals to connect with the victim's *right-brain* state (nonverbal) at this point: to communicative facial expressions, tone of voice, empathize, comfort, pause to observe, *and* listen. *Then,* re-direct with the left brain by using gentle words laced with authority on the subject, logical explanations, the message of overcoming, identifying and setting boundaries, processing solutions, and planning for resolution of the victim's distress.

The victim is presenting herself with right-brain dominance because of her past and current memories. The victim is essentially disclosing that she's *stuck* on her pathological memories and functioning out of those memories (images) because that's where her focus has been. As of now, this has consumed her entire world. Memories are shaping her present—she's bringing her past experiences forward into the present. The professional's task at hand is to guide her into getting herself unstuck from her memories and reactive "can't do it" state. One way to redirect her focus is to introduce the new experience of processing in a safe environment (remember, her brain can change from new experience). The victim, being able to process by talking about her mind and what it's thinking, will develop her own mind. Ask the victim (once brain functioning has been explained to her) to take a moment to jot down what she can do immediately to develop her own whole brain perspective. This note-to-self will aid the victim in organizing her left and right brain thoughts and in redirecting her thoughts to a balanced left and right brain way of thinking.

RECONCILIATION ADVISOR VS. THE PROFESSIONAL

The professional's and victim's co-regulation goal needs to be developing a new, healthy memory bank. The victim has to be taught that she can deposit into her new memory bank new, positive thoughts and experiences and withdraw negative, painful experiences along the way. She has to learn to deposit and talk to her brain and say, "You're not that abused woman anymore; you're an *Overcomer* now." Neurologically, when she learns to do this, she will be able to stop the amygdala from flooding and from keeping her MPFC from operating and developing. Once the MPFC is developing through the therapeutic relationship (and through other relationships), the victim's struggles, and diagnosis can be transformed into opportunities to rewire the brain. Intentional clinical and relational experiences shape brain wiring. Repeated positive relational experiences can transform and structure the brain's integration and can change the brain to be more resilient and less reactive.

The mission and vision goal of CBT with a victim of abuse is to train her to develop a whole-brain perspective (left and right brain) on both her life and the lives of others. This goal can be accomplished by teaching the victim about her brain, using interventions that lay the groundwork for her brain integration, and by the professional monitoring his personal and clinical malleable brain development. A professional has to be able to take more than a moment to jot down what he can do to develop his own whole-brain perspective. Through the co-regulation process, a professional is invariably exposed to the unavoidable self-integration (self-regulation). As the professional works toward providing integration strategies, the professional's own brain becomes *even more* integrated.

At whatever state of the brain integration process that the victim is in, the professional is always responsible for demonstrating sensitivity to the victim's internal state so that at all times, she feels *understood* in a meaningful way. When the professional is able to reflect on the victim's brain state and provide her with empathy and insight, she will respond to the professional's question of, "What do you *need* in order to make it right?" with reduced anxiety and offer what she *can* do. That is to say, she will be provided with an opportunity to use *mindfulness* (purposely paying attention to her thoughts, feelings, and actions) and opportunities to regulate her next bodily actions. As is self-explanatory, all of these brain development changes don't occur overnight, but the important factor is that the victim is given ample opportunity to practice voicing and doing things the right way—through integrated brain thinking and doing. What we do as a professional and as a human being in society is of significant influence and *does* matter profoundly as to how we can powerfully affect others' brains.

Speaking of how we are able to influence one another's brains (negatively and positively), what if the victim or *Overcomer* has a deficit in brain processing? After all, abuse trauma can negatively change the brain. How does abuse trauma change the brain? Through brain damage: Traumatic Brain Injury (TBI). Studies have concluded that victims of abuse are at high risk for also living with brain injury, while in the relationship with the abuser and after the relationship ends. How does TBI come into play with victims of abuse? What is a helper's treatment approach when working on abuse trauma that also has the manifestations of TBI?

Let's first discuss the fragility of the brain. When discussing brain trauma most of us have heard of our brain being compared to the texture of a raw egg's soft interior and its exterior used as an analogy for the hardness of our skull. Regardless of the egg's hard, protective exterior, the interior of the egg can still be damaged if care is not taken. If an egg is shaken, its interior substance will change, even if the exterior hard surface remains intact. Just like the egg's interior and exterior can be damaged by careless or intentional mishandling, our brain can be damaged by the sudden striking of its soft substance against the skull (the cranium which has interior sharp edges and ridges).

This is especially true of the brain because the brain consists of nerve fibers that communicate signals and messages throughout various parts of the brain and our bodily organs. The brain being struck against the interior hard surface of the skull may cause the brain tissue to swell and individual nerve cells or fibers to twist, bruise, bleed, stretch, tear, and/or shear. The brain fibers and structures may become damaged in more than one location of the brain. When the brain is traumatized (injured) its communication is disturbed; it cannot communicate effectively. Trauma in the brain can result in cognitive, emotional, behavioral, and physical symptoms. Some brain trauma affects a person's ability to perform daily living functions.

There are visible signs of TBI ranging from mild to severe: difficulty expressing herself or communicating, headaches, nausea, exhaustion, sleep disorder, cognitive fatigue, memory lapses/loss, speech impediment, vision impairment, seizures, sensitivity to light or sound, dizziness, depression/mood swings, anxiety, challenges with decision-making or concentration, inability to multitask, impulsivity, and/or out of control anger/aggression. However, TBI is not a diagnosis that is readily visible in symptomology because there are other causes assigned to emotional, behavioral, and physical symptoms; interior brain damage is not visible. For example, after an abusive episode, a victim may appear and feel the same physically but still have brain damage sustained by the abusive incident(s). In view of this reality, it is possible for a victim of abuse to be experiencing TBI symptoms that are related to the abuse, but be incognizant of this fact. This is one of the reasons why victims of abuse trauma are not screened for TBI (in addition to professionals not seeing the symptoms or not evaluating victims for TBI). Some studies have shown that even when symptoms that meet the criteria for the TBI diagnosis are visible in victims, clinics and hospitals fail to order a screening test.

A lot of research and training has been done to treat athletes and military veterans diagnosed with traumatic brain injury (TBI) but much work remains to be done in the area of screening and treating victims of abuse who also suffer from the same diagnosis. In victim abuse trauma it's rare that the helper is able to identify (unless trained on brain trauma) the dynamics or events leading to or causing brain damage but the brain injury is identifiable (with proper assessment tools). The etiology may not be disclosed by the victim but the helper is able to listen to or observe some of the consequences of TBI. A simple one page questionnaire that can serve as an inventory assessment tool to listen for and identify symptoms of TBI is the HELPS Screening Tool (see Resources). The results of this screening can be helpful to determinate if a victim of abuse needs to be referred for a neurological assessment.

Brain damage is missed in victims of abuse primarily because of a lack of awareness and education on the fact that TBI is a possible diagnosis with abuse victims. How is TBI possible in victims of abuse? A large percentage of victims of abuse are shaken (such as the shaking of an egg), punched, shoved, or pushed and may have fallen and hit their heads, or are directly hit on the head. It's estimated by various studies that over ninety percent of all abuse injuries involve the facial, neck, and head regions of the body. Some abuse victims pass out and may lose consciousness especially if strangulation is attempted and oxygen is not delivered to the brain—which damages the brain. This absence of oxygen kills brain cells and brain injury occurs. Even if the victim is conscious but loses blood flow, deprivation of blood circulation damages the brain (because oxygen travels via the blood and a decrease in blood flow can injure the brain).

RECONCILIATION ADVISOR VS. THE PROFESSIONAL

Many victims suffer from their face and head being pushed against an object or objects being thrown at them, or they're slammed against walls or furniture resulting in closed-head injuries (the skull remains intact). Closed-head injuries can impair cognitive skills and cause long term psychiatric or physical disorders. Most victims experience multiple incidents of brain damage that goes undetected. Untreated incidents of brain injury, and in some cases, one injury after another without recovery and healing from the previous injury may lead to permanent brain damage. This is why it's important for both the helper and the victim to assess the symptoms together early on when the victim presents herself for treatment because invisible brain injury has to be diagnosed. For example, if the victim is experiencing vocal cord dysfunction (VCD), how does one know that when she wants to speak or scream and she's unable to use her vocal cords that it's because she's constantly being frightened, experiencing anxiety, or that it's a result of chronic psychosocial stressors or brain damage, or a combination of all of the above? Undiagnosed or misdiagnosed TBI leads to unsupported victims with untreated brain injuries that can continue to deteriorate the brain, leading to psychiatric and physical disabilities, and early death.

Since most often there are no visible TBI lesions through CT or MRI radiology because those are not the most reliable screens to display the microscopic stretch marks and tear lines of the nerve cells; it's mandatory that a higher sensitivity instrument be used, like Diffusion Tensor Imaging (DTI) which can pick up evidence of hidden brain injuries. Or, a Single Photon Emission Computed Tomography (SPECT) is a good choice because shearing of the brain can be seen and it also provides a road map as to a history of the victim's brain condition and current functioning; SPECT targets her brain blood flow and activity. The SPECT will not just make the structures of her brain visible but it serves like a report card on *if* or at what level her brain has been injured by emotional (childhood?) and or the current physical level of trauma to the brain. A neurological assessment of the victim's brain is necessary in addition to documenting her reported symptoms. Yes, she's reporting classic brain damage symptoms of abuse, but victim brains vary; just like with all human brains, they vary in size, blood flow, and activity.

Working with a recovered victim of abuse that has TBI requires a helper to obtain the knowledge and training skills in order to practice and provide trauma-informed care. It's important to understand the specific brain injuries that are impacting her life. Working with TBI necessitates an extra dose of empathy and patience wrapped in respect for her right to self-determination. All of the symptoms affect the dynamics of the scheduled sessions. There may be a loss of memory, reduced communication skills, embarrassment for inability to perform daily living skills, she may feel misunderstood or judged negatively for her appearance and functioning, have difficulty processing and staying focused or attentive, be defensive, grieve over the loss of her former self, have a reduced self-esteem, and a general inability to conduct day-to-day tasks. It's your role to assist her in rebuilding herself cognitively and as a new person, in her new normal, so that she may be able to live her life to the fullest and the best that it can be.

Some of the problems that existed while the victim was still in the abusive relationship may re-surface after TBI: poor insight and judgment, confusion, depression, foggy thinking, suicidal ideation/attempts, vigilant, anxiety, feeling unsafe, unable to adapt to sudden changes or complete the multiple changes, difficulty maintaining social or important commitments, isolation, low tolerance for frustration, and functioning in irritable or aggressive moods. It's important to be objective regarding the fact that emotional abuse trauma may induce symptoms of

RECONCILIATION ADVISOR VS. THE PROFESSIONAL

oppositional and sometimes aggressive behaviors, as well as TBI being the culprit. Regardless of the etiology of all the symptoms of aggression or violence for both the victim and the abuser, whether it is TBI or abuse trauma related, TBI may contribute to aggressive patterns of behavior but it is not the cause of aggression or violence. There's no cause or excuse for abuse.

Working with a recovered victim of abuse that has TBI can mean regression into her victim stage as when she experienced difficulty assessing when she was in danger, or developing goals or even planning her day-to-day activities. She may need assistance with remembering to maintain her post-escape safety plan; assistance with outlining the short and long term pros and cons and consequences of her decisions; legal assistance resources to maintain custody or visitation of her children; financial planning connections to support herself independent of her former abuser; guidance on reconnecting with her resources; connecting her to advocacy for her TBI and instructions for remaining committed to her *Overcomer* lifestyle; she may need help with resources to find living arrangements that can best suit her daily needs while living with TBI. Your supportive role is to provide her with respect for her dignity by giving her useful feedback regarding her TBI. Inform her of realistic diagnosis problems that are evident in her and what can be encountered in future interactions, while all the while identifying and leading her to use her strengths. When she's about to enter the job market, school, or the criminal justice system, she may be faced with the abused woman discrimination which most TBI victims experience; because they are perceived as unable to communicate, confused, anxious, emotionally out of sorts, disorganized in the presentation of documentation or evidence, and unbalanced in temperament. TBI symptoms may lead to a prospective employer, school, or the judicial system misunderstanding or mislabeling her into a mental health diagnosis and falsely discrediting her as a responsible employee, parent, student, or valid witness to her own or others' cases.

It is to her advantage and all of those that work with her as prospective employers, instructors, advocates, service providers, and the judicial system to become sensitively informed about victim abuse trauma and to increase their awareness of the possibility and consequences of TBI. Better treatment outcomes result from properly diagnosed victims of abuse. For example, safety planning with a victim of TBI is approached differently, than with a victim who has abuse trauma but does not have TBI. Let's do an overview of what Safety Planning with a TBI recovering abuse victim can look like.

Safety planning with a TBI recovering victim of abuse (Overcomer) requires increased structure and organization but with fewer details for the process.

1. Use an alphabetic or numeric system to organize the safety steps in the order of her plan, A, B, C, or first, second, third step, etc.
2. Plans have to be frequently repeated to compensate for depression/anxiety, lack of self-initiative, lower motivation, severe indecisiveness, memory loss, and lack of follow-through.
3. Encourage her to be realistic about what and how much she is able to accomplish in one day, due to *rest* being an alleviator to her fatigue, depression, and a mood balancer.
4. Role-play with her before she's scheduled for job interviews, legal or other stressful appointments.
5. Periodically evaluate what her needs are in order to manage her TBI and maintain her freedom from abuse (supported job, vehicle, service animal/assistive devices, rehabilitation therapies, online and community support groups, group or independent living skills home care/family care).

6. Routinely review post escape safety planning and revise as necessary for improvements.
7. Teach her simple memory techniques such as setting phone alarms or text message self-reminders to create memory lists/post-it notes, journal, and using a pegging memory system by attaching a word/number/vision to an already known item/thought she wants to remember.
8. Repeatedly remind her that aerobic exercise builds the size of her hippocampus (thereby boosting memory and clear thinking). Assign brain exercises to train and strengthen her prefrontal cortex.
9. Use your truth-telling toolbox of cognitive, reality-based therapies, and spiritual encouragement to treat neuropsychiatric symptoms and prevent further brain injury.
10. Remind her to visit the Brain Injury Resource Center at www.braininjury.com in order to keep herself updated on her tools for self-advocacy and to use the online links to obtain support, as well as add the Head Injury Hotline phone number 206-621-8558 to her emergency contacts.

What if the victim's neurological assessment and scan results indicate no brain damage? There still remains the fact that we all experience positive and negative stressors in our daily life, however, prolonged chronic stress leads to brain damage. Untreated chronic stress places the abuse victim and recovered victim at risk for mental and physical illnesses. If she has already been diagnosed with either an emotional or physical illness, prolonged stress will change the functioning and structures of her brain, thereby increasing short-term and long-term symptoms and consequences.

Research has found that chronic stress can kill new vital neurons which are formed in the hippocampus (the part of the brain that's responsible for emotion, learning, and memory). Both child and adult studies have found that ongoing high stress levels can put the brain at risk for brain shrinkage in the various brain regions including the brain parts that regulate emotions, metabolism, and memory. This is a clinical concern because brain shrinkage and a decrease in brain activity in the frontal temporal lobe are typically seen in patients diagnosed with Alzheimer's and dementia.

Studies which fully demonstrate the implications of abuse trauma are the multiple researches done on child neglect and abuse of every type, which conclude that abuse trauma results in permanently changing the developing brain. The brains of happy, functioning children have been compared with abused, dysfunctional children's brains of the same age. Neurological images reveal abused children's brains are smaller in size compared to the normal size for the same age, happy, functioning child's brain. Such brain structure changes have been found to place abused children at high risk for emotional and psychiatric challenges as adults (mental and substance abuse disorders). It is not uncommon for victims of abuse trauma to use prescription or illegal drugs to in-their-own-way cope and medicate their self (if they choose that path).

Given the data about childhood abuse causing brain development shrinkage and damage to brain structure (and having already established that the brain continues to develop throughout a human's lifespan) it is clear that adult victims of abuse are at risk for brain damage. Abuse trauma can have significant enduring structural effects on the brain. How is an adult victim of abuse expected to make sound rational decisions when her brain has been or is being impaired in the brain regions that operate emotions, cognitive processing, social functioning, impulses, and self-regulation?

In comes you—the helper. Without articulating every study done on abuse and brain damage (which you can easily access), the data on abuse trauma concludes that brain recovery is possible. If treatment for brain damage is combined with: a comprehension about the history of the abuse and an understanding of the current symptoms after the abuse; the right treatment modalities and rehabilitation; TBI resources; supportive empathy; and clinical nurturing; this approach can restore a brain back to health at its highest level of functioning (level of functioning will depend on the level of damage). For optimal brain function, the goal of the helper and the recovering abuse trauma victim is to work together toward healthy development of the neural systems.

However, it's imperative to note that no two victims are alike. Victims may have suffered the identical abuser tactics and have similar symptoms, but a brain damage assessment should never be preceded by a conclusion based on reported symptoms and matching those symptoms to a research study or a manual of psychiatric disorders that lists brain disorders with codes that label the patient with a diagnosis. It's crucial that a victim of abuse receive an individualized initial intake with a final assessment (diagnosis) that incorporates biological findings obtained from a physical exam and brain scan. Treatment strategies must be based on the emotional, physical, and neurological test results. Treatment modalities must be developed and formulated based on the condition of her brain. Does she have a good, full (even), active, or overactive (high) or underactive (low) brain activity level?

There could be or there might not be a traumatic brain injury. Is the TBI mild, moderate, or severe? The only way to know if there's a TBI is to obtain the results from a brain scan and then proceed with a personalized brain rehabilitation treatment—if brain trauma is diagnosed. You won't be the only helper involved; TBI requires a head-trauma treatment team. Depending on the level of brain injury, there may be minimal intervention needed or perhaps pharmacology, EEG biofeedback, surgery, vision, speech, physical, vocational, or occupational therapies used to rehabilitate the brain back into independent functioning with self-care at home and in the community. Rehabilitation therapies prepare for adapting to and managing if there are any lingering neurological deficits and permanent disabilities.

TBI prognosis will vary and depends on: the level of injury, the lesions found, the region of the brain damage, access to specialized treatment, victim's age, health habits, coping strategies, genetic pre-disposition, IQ prior to injury, victim's personality profile, spiritual, family, social and economic support systems, and the level of the victim's involvement in recovery. The ultimate goal is to restore her former identity but with an improved self and a healthier brain. Brain-healthy habits are central to a victim's holistic healing. (Brain-healthy habits are spelled out in *Volume II Part I Overcoming Abuse: Embracing Peace Your Encyclopedic Guide to Freedom from Abuse.*) When a victim's brain is healed from the trauma of abuse she is more likely to never return to an abusive lifestyle. The right assessment and brain scan with a treatment team approach equals a significantly recovered victim (*Overcomer*) that can live an empowered, abundant life!

Combining CBT, Reality Therapy, & Neurology
If Cognitive Behavioral Therapy (CBT) is combined with *Reality Therapy* (RT), it produces added results because both therapies take a hands-on approach to working in the present so as to empower the patient with the ability to create her own future well-being. This, in turn, creates neurological changes in her brain. RT is especially therapeutic for victims because it focuses on choice and change. RT emphasizes the principle that, regardless of people being a product of their past social upbringing and past experiences, they don't have to live in the captivity of their past. RT is synonymous with Choice Theory, which posits that nearly

all mental health illnesses are based on being unhappy and dissatisfied but that humans are able to learn to choose healthier alternate behaviors that can lead them to a happier, satisfying life.

RT is a Choice Theory, based on a process, which helps victims to educate themselves on their choices. CBT and Reality Therapy uses the premise that propels a victim to become an *Overcomer*; all we can do for another person is to provide the information. The only behavior we can control is our own. CBT and RT are indeed therapies of hope because they are based on the belief that a victim may be a product of her past victimization, *but* she doesn't have to go on being its victim. The most important part for a professional to always keep in mind is that when working with a victim, even *one* intervention, no matter how simple, can have a lifetime neurological impact on her brain and functioning!

Post-Traumatic Stress Disorder (PTSD)
Some victims who experience *prolonged* abuse are likely to suffer from Post-Traumatic Stress Disorder (PTSD). PTSD is a syndrome known to accompany the sufferings of victims of abuse. In the past decades, combat veterans have been assigned the PTSD diagnosis. Through the process of diagnosing combat veterans, it was deduced that the syndrome observed in victims of incest, rape, and family violence is the very same syndrome observed in survivors of war. PTSD and the invisible wounds of war are also visible in victims of abuse. There is one difference between the victim of abuse and the war veteran's PTSD, and that is that when the veteran returns home, the problem of needing protection and safety does not typically exist for the war veteran.

With war veterans, usually their family, friends, and veteran's resources are available to provide welcoming relationships and support. In victim abuse, the victim is always at risk for another attack and needs safety and protection from her abuser. Usually, the victim is forced into isolation by her abuser; supportive family, friends, and resources are *not* always readily available. This lack of support (isolation) which the victim experiences is the main reason that the confusion and despair she endures escalates into trauma, because if she would have had access to an encouraging and supportive environment in those periods of abuse, she could have been spared of the worst of her PTSD symptoms.

A victim of abuse undergoing PTSD is not based on a single episode of abuse; it is based on being under the *prolonged* dominion of the abuser whereby repeated trauma occurs. This repetitive trauma reoccurs because she is not free to leave her abuser and is under his coercive control, such as a prisoner of war (POW). The difference being that most POWs are recognized in their captivity by our society, whereas victims of home captivity usually go unrecognized. Even the place of captivity for a POW has visible, physical constraints like cell bars, barbed wire fences, or locked dungeons; however, an abused victim's home is rarely seen as the same constraining prison of a POW with its invisible, physical barriers that don't allow her to escape. A victim of abuse is a prisoner of home—a POH—without parole. The extremely powerful invisible balls, chains, and barriers, which imprison victims of abuse, are their docile dependency, their servility to the abuser, their endurance of the threat of brutality and physical force, and their legal, social, and economic stratifications and imposed-upon subordination.

These powerful, invisible barriers result in the victim establishing a special type of relationship with her abuser. The abuser uses a combination of manipulation, enticement, intimidation, threats, and forces so as to become the most influential person in the victim's life. At this point, the victim's mentality is broken and shaped by the belief system and actions of the abuser. The abuser does not allow the victim to know *anything* about his mentality; he is contemptuous when she seeks to understand his

RECONCILIATION ADVISOR VS. THE PROFESSIONAL

belief system, and he does not seek to be understood because he does not perceive that there's anything wrong with his thinking or actions.

Most victims that are exposed to prolonged, recurrent abusive trauma develop a treacherous, progressive PTSD that captures and attempts to destroy the victim's person. Whereas a victim of a single act of abuse may feel unlike her normal self, the victim of recurrent trauma may feel a sense of disintegration as if she has been unequivocally changed, and she may even feel that she is now irreversible and has lost her sense of self. This prolonged abusive trauma alters the victim's self-identity. The victim's image of herself (Spirit, Mind, and Body) and her own images of others (her values and coherent sense of purpose) have been seized and consistently, inhumanely broken down.

Even after the victim is apart from the abuser, she cannot readily assume her pre-abuse identity. Her new identity post-abuse, *even in freedom,* includes the traumatic memory of her captured self. The image of her Spirit, Mind, and Body still includes the idea that she can be controlled and desecrated. Her memory, even after escaping abuse, includes the vision of herself having been a person who lost herself to her abuser and others. Her new knowledge of her past self includes her moral ideals pre-abuse, which now coexist with the capacity within the abuser for sinfulness, within others and within herself. When under extreme stress, the recovering victim may feel tremendous, burdened shame and guilt for having betrayed her own moral principles or having disowned significant others and now has to live with a memory of herself as an accomplice to the abuser. This, in turn, re-traumatizes the recovering victim through re-visiting her broken person whom she loathes and sees as a complete failure.

At this stage, the victim is suffering from Moral Injury (MI), a trauma-related syndrome that was first researched by psychiatrist and professor Jonathan Shay and colleagues. They studied military and veteran patients that reported symptoms based on their perceptions of moral injustices. MI can also be experienced by the victim who has been transgressed against by being treated inhumanely and violated in love, health, and safety or who has seen or experienced violence or immoral acts. MI is present in the victim if there has been a betrayal of what she believes is morally right by someone in authority who is trusted (the abuser). MI is the violation of the victim's values and standards. It's the transgression against the victim that injures her moral conscience, which produces deeply-imbedded emotional shame. Other symptoms include loss of trust, anxiety, depression, guilt, anger, self-harm, suicidal ideation, addictions, relationship conflicts, isolation, self-sabotage, flashbacks or reenactment of moral conflict with others, and loss of meaning in life. The victim can feel both responsible for failing to prevent the violations and bearing witness to the pain of the transgressions against herself and her children as well as anger toward her perpetrating abuser for failing to stop the suffering.

From a spiritual perspective, MI has been researched by Rita Nakashima and Gabriella Lettini. They define MI as "souls in anguish" and do not diagnose it as a psychological disorder. They emphasize the lost sense of humanity after the victim's deeply-held moral beliefs have been transgressed. The focus of their work is more on MI as normal human responses to abnormal, traumatic events. MI is one of the reasons total redemption is necessary in order for a victim's "soul in anguish" to fully recover, heal, and move into the position of an *Overcomer*.

Sustained, incessant abuse results in multiple losses for a victim (in addition to her moral image), which can result in a steadfast, progressive depression. Long-term depression is a common diagnosis in clinical studies of chronically traumatized persons. Prolonged trauma may exacerbate symptoms of depression to

RECONCILIATION ADVISOR VS. THE PROFESSIONAL

a vegetative state. A victim's self-image is debased as a result of the ongoing trauma; this is the foundation for symptoms of depression. Some of the depression is symptomatic of the victim's inability to express her anger toward her abuser for fear of her safety being compromised. Withholding her feelings of anger for having been in captivity for so long and being unable to talk to her abuser about her oppressed state increases her depression (because of her silent rage toward her abuser). When a victim denies her abuse circumstances and allows those episodes to pile up within her, depression sets in. The victim's relief from depression can only happen if she does not allow her emotional pain from the abuse to accumulate. Whether it's the unresolved abuse buried into the victim's subconscious mind or ongoing worry, the end result will be bitter sadness. The only solution for the depression leaving is for the victim to problem-solve whatever she can resolve and to refuse to accept whatever she is unable to solve.

Despite the victim having been apart from the abuser and having had no contact with him, she may continue to fear his vengeance and may be cautious about vocalizing *any* anger toward him. This invariably sets up the victim to be left with rage that has been unexpressed and remains there toward the abuser and others who refused to help her out of her abusive relationship. Left untreated, this PTSD symptom of rage may exhibit itself on others, which will then perpetuate the depressive, isolated state of the recovering victim. This can then preclude her from restoring former relationships and from building new ones. Isolation can further discourage the victim who has been chronically traumatized into a loss of faith and into a depressed state that may entertain hopelessness. When hopelessness enters the human mind, there's a risk for the depression to deepen into a risk for suicide.

Depression is a common, serious clinical illness which complicates the PTSD symptoms of a victim. There is a tendency to misdiagnose victims of abuse as patients who have personality or other mental disorders. The victim is presumed to have some form of underlying psychopathology. This presumption takes place even when it is well-known that any healthy individuals who experience a crisis that has involved trauma are no longer the healthy individuals they were prior to their traumatic event when they are recovering from the crisis. The fact is that prolonged abuse causes deep harm to the Spirit, Mind, and Body. This tendency to misdiagnose the victim by assigning her a personality or mental disorder or blaming her for her abuse only interferes with the recognition of her PTSD diagnosis.

This intense post-traumatic stress factor (whether solely emotional or combined emotional and physical abuse) plays a role in the victim's life while in the presence of the abuser and while apart from the abuser. A victim with PTSD keeps returning to her blistering, oozing wounds and haunting memories. If the victim is struggling with PTSD symptoms while in and outside of therapy sessions, it distracts her from developing a safety plan and from problem-solving her victim role because the focus is on the interfering thoughts and anxiety. Once trust levels have been established with her, an exercise that is useful for some victims that experience PTSD fear or anxiety is meditation-relaxation therapy, such as Guided Imagery (GI). GI ameliorates PTSD symptoms. The GI visualization techniques are useful to help the victim imagine herself being at a pleasant location of her choice, in a safe and relaxed state. The victim may say that she can't think of any safe place, but tell her that she does have her Spirit within her as a place of refuge and that her Spirit is larger than any suffering. If she's unable or unwilling to select a safe place, suggest and guide her to a tranquil nature scene. GI includes a deep breathing exercise with muscle relaxation,

RECONCILIATION ADVISOR VS. THE PROFESSIONAL

tension-releasing, soft music, and voiced descriptive graphic-imaged scenery (which evoke feelings of strength and safety).

Guided Imagery is not a mystical exercise. The purpose is to re-direct the victim back to her healthy identity, back to where she wants to go (her peaceful self). The goal of this technique is to reduce, not increase, her anxiety and stress levels. She can close her eyes and listen to her own recorded or the professional's low-spoken, soothing voiced messages that are playing her affirmations, helping her to voice and visualize her fear leaving her, and thinking of being safe with peace of mind. For best results, she can engage in this exercise for fifteen to thirty minutes while receiving her positive messages about the state of her Spirit, Mind, and Body. Some victims of abuse trauma prefer to keep their eyes open at first, which is acceptable; allow her to set her own pace with the exercise. She will at some point become totally focused and absorbed by her visualization of herself; this will deepen progressively and leave her in a relaxed, peaceful, calm state.

The Guided Imagery must end with an instructive message, such as, "Gradually open your eyes, and gently stretch your body. Notice how refreshed your mind feels. Once you feel back to your usual, alert state, continue your day feeling relaxed and at peace." If she prefers not to create her own GI recorded meditation exercises, there are Guided Imagery Audio CDs for Post-Traumatic Stress available for purchase on the internet; all she would have to do is select a place where she would not be interrupted, and simply listen. For GI to be effective, it requires willingness, motivation, and consistent, intentional listening. Ultimately, Guided Imagery exercises can aid the victim in taking control of the traumatic images in her mind.

Treating PTSD with Exposure Therapy

Whenever a human being experiences abuse, the normal survival instinct is to respond with an attempt to deflect attention from being traumatized and bury these thoughts from consciousness; abuse, however, refuses such denial and burial. This *survival mode* (attempt to bury/deny in the mind) *does not* work to recover and to heal from abuse. This is where Exposure Therapy (ET) (a form of CBT) is most useful; the victim has to be walked through and gradually exposed to her past abuse. This is not psychoanalytical; it is just *processing* the abuse with a victim suffering from PTSD.

Remembering the brutality of the abuse and being truthful about the abhorrent incidents of abuse are the prerequisites for the recovery of the victim from victimization into individual healing as an *Overcomer* of her abuse. This is an extremely sensitive time for both the helper and the victim, but most of the responsibility is upon the helper to use *mindful* words when treating with ET. Any impatient, insensitive words can be dispiriting to a victim whose symptoms keep recurring.

The victim's symptoms need to be validated; she needs to know that such symptoms (fear, anxiety, panic) are debilitating and that they're real, physical symptoms. She has to be reassured that such a frightened state can be treated effectively. It is when the victim and her support system admit to the truth of her ghastly abuse and her symptoms that the *Overcomer* path becomes a reality. It is the letting go of the silence and the cooperation from the victim not to bury the abuse or her symptoms that turns the traumatic events of the abuse from symptoms of abuse into real life experiences that require recovery and healing.

The PTSD recovery process for a victim of abuse has three developmental phases of recovery: **Phase I**, *Creating a Safe Environment;* **Phase II**, *Recreating the Story of the Trauma;* **Phase**

RECONCILIATION ADVISOR VS. THE PROFESSIONAL

III, Reestablishing the Relationship Between the Former Victim and her Society:

Phase I *Creating a Safe Environment*—This reveals a victim's trauma as it can be seen through her nonverbal communication. Her entire physiognomy depicts her unspeakable journey. The victim's eyes, if you look closely at her pupils, tell a story of her powerlessness and fear. Her affliction is visible by the terror in her eyes and her demeanor as she exhibits a composure that infers she has been rendered helpless by her abuser. There are stories beyond her eyes, inside of her, within her soul. These are stories that she may have blocked because these stories are too heinous to recall—too overwhelming to re-experience—and talk about. Those are secret stories, which she may be willing to talk about if only she could be guaranteed a protective environment, a place of safety. Professionals are in a position to offer this confidential, protective environment and relationship and to guide the victim, such as through the creation of a SEP.

Phase II *Recreating the Story of the Trauma*—This entails helping the victim to engage in rebuilding her life story. Helping her to reconstruct her life involves processing her trauma while simultaneously guiding her to breaking ground on her new foundation. There is no way around processing her trauma if the goal of fully relieving PTSD symptoms is to be accomplished. This is a difficult but necessary therapeutic intervention because victims traumatized by abuse become adept at suppressing painful thoughts and minimizing their hurt, which keeps them at a denial stage; it's a strategy they have always used to alter their unbearable, real circumstances into a comfort zone. Research indicates that the mere effort of *telling their story* within the context of a protective relationship that offers a safe environment produces change in the abnormal processing occurring in the brain with traumatic memory.

Many of the major symptoms of PTSD can be reversed through the use of words—by processing the traumatic story that induces terror. Reducing PTSD symptoms is the short-term goal. Re-writing the victim's script into her story by transforming it into an *Overcomer* script (an *Overcomer* story) is the long-term goal in this phase. Once the victim has thoroughly processed her story as normal memory does, her story now transforms the traumatic memory so that it can be integrated into her very own *Overcomer* life story. On the contrary, if the victim does not break her silence, then the memory remains as a traumatic memory does, wordless and unchanged with powerful, unexpressed emotions and haunting recollections. The victim must work to understand her past in order to reclaim her present and develop her future. However, the choice to confront and process the horrific events of her past which have resulted in PTSD symptoms always rests with the victim. A victim lets go of her past when she decides that she is done with it. She is finished with her victim role; she has grieved and moved on. She's now complete with her enriched life as a new *Overcomer*. She has been transformed and has a new life story!

Phase III *Reestablishing the Relationship Between the Former Victim and her Society*—This involves targeting the newfound freedom from terror and the trust that the victim has been developing to reestablish the victim as an *Overcomer* in her community and within society as a whole. This newfound empowerment gives the formerly traumatized victim meaning and purpose as an *Overcomer*. She now moves from her disconnected isolation and uses this new energetic strength as an opportunity to build relationships, reconnecting her own life with a sense of control.

In order to conquer PTSD, the victim *has to* get to a position in her life whereby she is able to examine her cognitive thought processes and evaluate how she responds or reacts to relationships and events that are a reminder of her trauma. This is not

RECONCILIATION ADVISOR VS. THE PROFESSIONAL

the same as processing ordinary, normal, day-to-day, healthy relationships and events. It is an intense process because the victim has been consistently exploited and exposed to information and situations that were beyond average, everyday, human experiences. She enters this phase with yet some apprehensions and doubts about the basics of trust in relationships.

Even though she has officially escaped or terminated her abusive relationship, it does not come humanly natural for her to reconcile with the community she has been isolated from or any other relationships that she held prior to her abuse. All of her relationships have been affected at a level that she can only view them through the lens of broken trust and at extreme levels of relating. Every relationship that she initiates or encounters is infected with the question of basic trust.

This is where the discernment and wisdom are gained about how PTSD plays a role in engaging the victim in either a survival or *Overcomer* mode as well as playing a destructive role in impeding her growth beyond the traumatic experiences. The victim now comprehends that it's normal for the human mind to periodically digress and recall imagery upon meeting a new person or circumstance that hints at a reminder of her trauma. She learns that it's our mind's way of *naturally* and *normally* re-integrating between past memory and the present. At the same time, she begins to identify past traumatic experiences that can no longer control her Spirit, Mind, and Body. She now uses spiritual support and therapeutic techniques that adhere to her newly transformed, re-written, PTSD-free, *Overcomer* script.

As articulated in the Exposure Therapy method, there are *three* phases of treatment. If you are a certified EMDR therapist (Eye Movement, Desensitization, and Reprocessing) and have an abused, traumatized victim with PTSD symptoms who would work well with the *eight* phases of EMDR and can benefit best from this treatment modality, then this would be a treatment of choice. The goals and approaches to Exposure therapy and EMDR are very similar: To fully process disturbing past memories, present disturbances, and to develop new, healthy experiences in order to organize, balance, and store all experiences appropriately in the brain. To alleviate and to stop future symptoms through the elimination of inappropriate emotions, unsound beliefs, and discarding unhealthy body sensations. Both Exposure Therapy and EMDR seek a PTSD outcome that will result in a healthy perspective, an understanding of the self, emotions, interactions, and the development of skills for present and future healthful behaviors.

PTSD Prognosis for the *Overcomer*
Does this mean that the *Overcomer* will never again suffer from PTSD symptoms of abuse? No. Recovery from PTSD is a lifetime health effort. It's the same as with any act of taking care of your well-being; it's not an every-so-often endeavor. It's like exercising to stay fit; you don't just exercise whenever you feel like it—you do it as a part of your everyday living. The resolved trauma will always be a part of the *Overcomer's* lifecycle; the impact of her past trauma can never be erased. As the *Overcomer* experiences new life transitions and reaches life milestones, there's always that chance that any of the PTSD phases of recovery that have been resolved can be re-visited as certain events bring her back to her traumatic memories. For example, while traveling to locations that bring back memories, weather similarities, a person's resemblance to the abuser, being exposed to extreme emotional, physical, sexual, and/or deprivation abuse through the media, certain odors or fragrances, music of the era whenever the victimization took place, family weddings, births, deaths, health changes, promotions, and retirement.

The awareness that PTSD symptoms can be reawakened does not by any means infer that the *Overcomer* is incapable of healing. It simply means that as with any human being, when the *Overcomer* is under increased positive or negative stress, her Spirit, Mind, and Body are likely to be affected. For the *Overcomer*, PTSD symptoms are likely to recur and resurface (from mild to severe), depending on the *Overcomer*'s ability to use the wisdom she gained through the principles that help her to empower her Spirit, Mind, and Body. The *Overcomer* can prevent PTSD symptom regression by being on top of her life transitions and milestones and managing her stress levels to help her to cope and remain strong and intact as an *Overcomer*. It is also important to note that there's no need for an *Overcomer* to feel weak or unrecovered if she feels a desire to return to therapy or to consult with a trusted individual whenever she believes she's re-experiencing PTSD symptoms; it's actually recommended that support be sought in order to alleviate and subside symptoms.

This is not to imply that the *Overcomer* needs to live a life of expectancy for the revival of her PTSD symptoms. It is just to say that this is an absolutely important part of the work of recovery, to have this awareness about traumatic memories and how they operate in a recovered person's life. Once aware of this information, the *Overcomer*'s main task is to give full attention to living her life to its fullest. The best indicator that the *Overcomer* has left the PTSD symptoms that once arrested her is her renewed quest for life and her enthusiasm for the development of healthy relationships. An *Overcomer*'s fear of living day to day is in the past, and her focus has to become basking in the present and looking to life in the future with gratitude and amazement at this wonderful life that she's now partaking in!

Group Therapy
Group Therapy is another useful treatment intervention with victims of abuse, at the discretion of the therapist, if the victim is a good candidate for group. This is usually dependent on what

phase of treatment she is in and if there are no known restrictions that would further impair her as a result of engaging in a group. Typically, group is indicated because there is healing that takes place when social bonds are made with others that have suffered the same pain. For instance, this is where she can feel safe to process not only her abusive episodes over her past months or years, but it also a place where she can talk about the good in her abuser(s) and what she misses about that. A group is a place that she can ventilate as many times as she feels her pain and grieve for as long as she needs to in a secure, supportive environment. The commonality of group members gives a sense of hope to the victim.

A support group reduces the victim's feelings of isolation, provides educational knowledge (through sharing, leaders teaching and/or workbook), and strengthens functioning-coping strategies. Group leaders and members can become a social network that concentrates on optimal living skills which promote living a mentally healthy life, holding one another accountable for their psychosocial lifestyle and any assignments that are prescribed in the group.

It is encouraging to a formerly isolated victim to discover that there are others that have been traumatized through abuse, that she's not alone with her hurt and that others have secret *abuse* stories that, through understanding and support, can become *Overcomer* stories. Simply associating with others that reassure her of confidentiality builds trusting relationships and provides an opportunity to ventilate the devastation, embarrassment, and blaming that she has had to endure. Other abused group members that are at more advanced phases of their recovery can share their past process and signal to the new *Overcomer* what is to come. Sometimes they share their survival strategies and ingenuity in their escape plans and maintenance skills to remain abuse-free.

RECONCILIATION ADVISOR VS. THE PROFESSIONAL

The universality of group members as a whole pulls together their experiences, thoughts, and feelings as they echo their private realities and integrate encouraging messages to one another. As they dialogue with one another, a group can also be beneficial in assisting the victim in re-writing her life script into an *Overcomer* script. Even the learning or relearning of social skills can take place in a group. A victim can become introspective in the safety of a group environment and examine how she interacts with others by making comparisons and learning to pursue appropriate, nurturing, and healthy relationships. Group members can become infomercials for one another while mirroring strength, hope, and providing a glimpse of what *peace* is like.

Group therapy is a reciprocating type of therapy. It helps the victim move away more quickly from focusing on herself and stepping out of her isolated comfort zone. This helps her to experience and develop empathy for others; she begins to increase her gratitude as she compares herself to others and becomes increasingly more tolerant of the differences in others. Group therapy allows for the expression of all feelings in the presence of others besides the therapist, including positive feelings of love and giving. The love and empathy she shares with others is reciprocated by others. This type of bonding and processing can occur in individual therapy or between friends and family that share and mirror one another, but it is enhanced in the context of a group that has the identical abusive past and is recovering from the same trauma. The strength, self-worth, boundaries, and autonomy gained are lifetime tools that the victim is able to incorporate into her new life as an *Overcomer* of abuse.

A group can act as an additional tool of empowerment for the recovering victim. This mutual relationship-building becomes a form of collective empowerment that holds one another accountable as comrades of the same traumatic experiences. There's a camaraderie that group members establish which is unlike non-therapeutic groups; the common bond of suffering does not stop them from supporting one another and contributing to the well-being of each member. The group does not allow for the revisiting of offensive behaviors from one member to another; instead, they gain strength through one another's recovery resources and foster the nurturing and independent dignity that they each deserve.

Now with all of the positives having been mentioned, as with any organized groups, there is also a downside to groups. In spite of some women that have left their abusive relationships rating their group therapy as their most effective source of help, groups can end just as quickly as they were organized. This then leads to aggravating group members' pain. There is a disappointing, destructive side to groups, just as there is hope to be had in developing and maintaining an active group. Unhealthy groups do erupt on occasion, which at that point become non-therapeutic because the dynamics of the abuse are re-experienced through conflicts between group members who take on the perpetrator, rescuer, and victim roles. This toxic acting out on behalf of the group members re-victimizes vulnerable group members, which contradicts the purpose of the group. The upheaval of group members is an indication that the group leader has not been clear about boundaries or rules or needs to re-clarify what the therapeutic goal of the group is.

It is the professional's responsibility to set structured group rules with consequences. Just like with individual therapy, the victim has to be protected in her right to self-determination; she's to be provided with the parallel process of her self-disclosure and that of others. She is to be listened to and supported, not judged or fixed by the leader or group members. It's the group leader's role to exercise ethical protection of each group member so that traumatic reenactment does not enter into the relationships that the group members share. Group cohesiveness is absolutely necessary for the success of an abuse recovery group; it's not any less relevant than for any other organized group. *Some* groups even go beyond verbal communication to express bonding and unity by establishing individual and group hug allowance. "Group hugging" often takes place after an intense group session; the group members huddle up and wrap their arms around one another, while the therapist wraps his arms around the entire group. These hugs communicate an expression of acceptance and bonding and provide brief moments of group togetherness.

Groups are not perfect, just like not all therapy is perfect. You're familiar with the group break up stories; you may have your own. Each group member has unique needs, capabilities, and varied perspectives on life. Nevertheless, in spite of these individual differences, we are all called (group or no group) to continue "endeavoring to keep the unity of the Spirit in the bond of peace" (Ephesians 4:3). We are also called to be as one, "That they all may be one, as You, Father, *are* in Me, and I in You; that they also may be one in Us" (John 17:21). When issues develop with one another, we are to respond, "with all lowliness and gentleness, with longsuffering, bearing with one another in love" (Ephesians 4:2). It is a group leader's obligation to intervene on and discourage disunity and to uphold group togetherness as one, such as Christ would. It's irrelevant if not all group members are Christians; in our Heavenly Father's eyes, we are all His children whom He created to be brothers and sisters in Christ. We are all linked through His love.

Christian Counseling
Christian individual and/or Christian group counseling is recommended with victims that do not use religion in unhealthy patterns. Some patients use uninformed biblical concepts or theological myths as their reasoning and justification for their

dysfunctional thinking and acting. There are some patients that have clinical diagnoses that would result in Christian counseling interventions further aggravating their mental states. For example, therapeutic discretion has to be of utmost importance in the case of, but not limited to, schizophrenia and psychosis; a careful balance has to be monitored as religious obsessions and ritualistic patterns can set in.

On the other hand, when victims combine their Spirit, Spiritual belief system, and Spiritual support with their therapeutic working goals, there are positive outcomes with long-lasting (eternal) effects. Christian counseling can become the victim's safety chain link fence of encouragement whereby the chain link of courage is made available from God, to her, and can be passed onto others in her life.

All therapists are familiar with the therapeutic intervention of *reframing* whereby we encourage the patient to shift her focus from her unproductive perspective (past frame of mind) and replace it with a more productive perspective (new frame of mind) of the situation or person. A therapeutic Christian counseling intervention that makes optimal use of *reframing* is a time when the patient is taught how to look at her life from *God's* perspective (renewing of the mind). God's Word can be instrumental in *reframing* by replacing the symptoms of the trauma of abuse with God's Word and His Scriptural promises. God is *real,* and in His Word (the Bible), He has provided over 7,000 Scriptural promises with His perspective—to be used in daily living.

Knowing that God's Word and promises are there and do not bounce back builds a foundation of faith, hope, and trust for the victim. Isaiah 55:11 says, "So shall My word be that goes forth from My mouth; It shall not return to me void. But it shall accomplish what I please, And it shall prosper *in the thing* for which I sent it."

RECONCILIATION ADVISOR VS. THE PROFESSIONAL

There have been studies which indicate that when patients engage in secular counseling as opposed to Christian counseling, there is a greater rate of recidivism. Regardless, the role of those who work with victims of abuse, whether on a secular or Christian counseling basis, ultimately becomes bona fide God-Work because it is, not by the worker's or victim's might nor power, that she is healed but by the Spirit of the Lord (Zechariah 4:6). I once heard a pastor say that in his counseling, he saw *fear* as Reality Therapy without God and *faith* as Reality Therapy with God. It has indeed been found that Combining CBT, Reality Therapy, and Group Therapy with Christian counseling makes for a powerful, increased rate of recovery for victims of abuse trauma.

Some health literature encourages the alignment of the *body*, *mind*, and *spirit* in that order, a holistic approach to our well-being. I believe in and am in favor of a holistic approach in the treatment of the patient; however, I elect to align a person's well-being in the order of the Spirit, Mind, and Body for reasons that I articulate in this part of the book.

Whenever I refer to the Spirit, I am not referring to secular spirituality. Secular spirituality adheres to the person's spirit being one without a relationship with God, the inner peace that comes from the individual. Secular spirituality focuses on humanistic qualities without divine intervention. Secular spirituality relies totally on the person nurturing their own thoughts, emotions, and actions without the supernatural power of God. The Spirit that I refer to and work with as a Christian therapist is the Holy Spirit, Who is capable of dwelling within each human being.

> "Do you not know that you are the temple of God and *that* the Spirit of God dwells in you? If anyone defiles the temple of God, God will destroy him.

For the temple of God is holy, which *temple* you are" (1 Corinthians 3:16-17).

I have worked with hundreds of patients in secular settings, and it has been my experience and that of my colleagues' that the rate of recidivism for patients that solely receive secular counseling is greater than those that receive Christian counseling incorporated into therapy sessions. When a patient works with a Christian therapist, that therapist works to empower the victim's Spirit (*Overcomer* faith, discernment, wisdom, eternal freedom), Mind (educate, develop awareness and insight), and Body (prioritized godly choices and actions, health care). A patient that works with a secular therapist receives the conventional therapy which traditional mental health practitioners offer.

Traditional mental health practitioners treat the mind, but this appears to be an incomplete treatment approach. It does not address the reality that the Spirit, Mind, and Body are not independent of one another. The Spirit, Mind, and Body are entwined; what influences one influences the others. There is much research that has been done through alternative medicine which indicates that there is a connection between disease and an imbalance among a patient's physical, emotional, spiritual, and environmental elements.

I am all for a holistic treatment plan for a victim or any other patient. But I am not in concurrence with the idea that people ought to look within themselves for human power as their own God. The reason for my support of a holistic approach is because holistic health doesn't just aim at setting an outcome goal for healing; it also focuses on teaching the skills of preventive care. Holistic health takes into account the whole person being treated: the social, psychological, and environmental factors that impact that person's health. Holistic professionals evaluate the body, mind, and spirit—evaluating and setting treatment goals that include influential factors such as body exercise, nutrition, and recreation. Conventional mental health professionals treat the mind and ignore the spiritual part of the being in relation to the mind and the body.

I elect to treat the Spirit, Mind, and Body; traditional therapists elect to treat symptoms with medication and psychoanalysis or other psychological theories. My preference is to look at what is causing the symptoms (etiology) and go beyond exploring the mind on the surface. I reserve recommending therapeutic drugs as a last option *unless* acute mental illness is the primary diagnosis and other treatment modalities have already been used. Recommending therapeutic drugs does not seek to resolve the underlying causes of the symptoms and only conceals the symptoms. While reducing symptoms with therapeutic drugs may be a temporary solution for *some* patients, it leaves serious underlying problems unresolved.

Another reason for us holistic mental health professionals finding conventional therapy with medication so abrasive is the fact that holistic strategies are designed to be wholesome approaches to healthful and nontoxic interventions for the patient. Holistic health promotes alignment in the patient's life whereby ultimately the patient may reach the goal of having a balance of harmony in their personal life and in relationship to others. Taking into account the Spirit, Mind, and Body in that order further allows the patient to actively participate in improving their life out of the realm of therapy. This holistic approach incorporates a balance into the therapeutic relationship that encourages the patient's autonomy. It educates the patient about their health issue and supports the practice of self-care in the treatment of that problem, empowering the patient to health, rather than relying on the therapist for permanent changes.

Holistic approaches encourage the alignment of the body, mind, spirit, separately. When the Spirit is not connected to the mind and body, the person feels defenseless with the disorder in their life. The Spirit is the driving force behind the mind *and* body, the driving force behind the person's life. When the mind and body are placed before the Spirit, they war against the person's Spirit. This is because of what Proverbs 23:7 says is the case: as a man thinks in his heart, so is he. Using the Spirit to renew the mind and discipline the body is essential—because the condition of the mind is the condition of one's heart. When one's heart is in order, so are one's thinking and actions. I elect to place the Spirit first when using a holistic approach in treatment because when the patient aligns their Spirit with their mind and body (in that order), that person's entire perspective on the self, others, and life changes! That person is now on their way to find their meaning and purpose for their life.

A word of serious caution—many individuals that have never had a personal encounter with the Spirit will be uneasy, and they may even act with an underlying allegation that the person experiencing the Spirit has fallen off the deep end! These individuals may even act offensively toward the person that has activated the Spirit within them and, out of ignorance, decide not to have any further discussions with the person on the matters of the Spirit. Regardless, these individuals need to be treated with respect in spite of their rejection of the Spirit's existence in humans. Some of these individuals may even defensively use sarcasm or mock the person who acknowledges the presence of the Spirit within them; they may call the person that's speaking, based on their perspective at the time, a "religious fanatic."

Each of us has a choice to either use the Spirit that lives within us or not—those individuals that have made a clear choice *not* to believe in the Spirit are to be treated in the same way as if they recognized the Spirit; it is just a matter of their being unable to understand the things of the Spirit at this time. The following Scriptures speak on how the Holy Spirit operates within us:

RECONCILIATION ADVISOR VS. THE PROFESSIONAL

"However, when He, the Spirit of truth, has come, He will guide you into all truth; for He will not speak on His own *authority*, but whatever He hears He will speak; and He will tell you things to come" (John 16:13). "But the natural man does not receive the things of the Spirit of God, for they are foolishness to him; nor can he know *them*, because they are spiritually discerned" (1 Corinthians 2:14). "For the message of the cross is foolishness to those who are perishing, but to us who are being saved it is the power of God" (1 Corinthians 1:18). Intellect is insufficient to understand spiritual matters because spiritual things can only be discerned by the Holy Spirit. When a person is led by the Holy Spirit, he/she is inspired into thinking, feeling, or action; inspiration comes from the Spirit. The word *inspiration* itself means to be *in spirit*.

How does any person—or the victim in front of you today—actively receive the Spirit of God within? It's one of the simplest acts that human beings can do—ask God (the Holy Spirit) to come into their hearts. All that person has to do is *believe*, and the power of the Holy Spirit will come! This then allows the person to start a new life with Christ in his or her heart. It's also called being born-again because the person now has embarked on a new life in Christ: "Therefore, if anyone *is* in Christ, *he is* a new creation; old things have passed away; behold, all things have become new" (2 Corinthians 5:17). Why in the world would a victim, or *any* human being for that matter, need to be born again? Why does *everyone* need to be born again? This question is actually answered in the Bible: "Jesus answered and said to him, I say to you, unless one is born again, he cannot see the kingdom of God" (John 3:3). What does it *mean* to be "born again?" To be born again is to be *Spiritually* born again, not as a religious ritualistic act but to be born again as Christ calls us to be, in the Bible. It means to have the Holy Spirit born in you.

Being born of the Spirit or being born again simply means that a person has an opportunity to be *born twice*. The first birth is the physical birth through the parents; the person is born into their family. The second birth is the person's Spiritual birth (born again). A Spiritual birth means being born again when Jesus Christ is born in the person and literally comes into his/her body to reside in the form of the Holy Spirit (the Spirit of God). Being born again is the same as when in the Bible, the apostles were filled with the Holy Spirit; Jesus said, "receive the Holy Spirit" (John 20:22). He will send His Spirit into the victim's heart so that she may grow only the fruit (including peace) that befits her *Overcomer* conversion. Once the Holy Spirit ascends upon her, God *recognizes her* from heaven as one of His children for whom He has granted a life of eternal *peace*! Being born again means she is Spiritually reborn into a new family—God's family. Being born again means she has now inherited becoming a part of one of the most privileged families on Earth—Christ's family!

Why should a victim consider that one of her tasks in her recovery from the trauma of abuse is to accept the Holy Spirit (Christ)? Because when a person *by faith* accepts Christ and His plan of salvation, that person is now born of God (born again), and this then accelerates the process and guarantees her becoming an *Overcomer*. God promises that those who have faith and believe that Christ is His Son who died for our sins can have *Overcomer* victory. "For whatever is born of God overcomes the world. And this is the victory that has overcome the world—our faith. Who is he who overcomes the world, but he who believes that Jesus is the Son of God?" (1 John 5:4-5). (More on this in Volume II Part II *Overcomer* Principles). The Holy Spirit has to be turned on in order to receive His power. If He is turned off, then He cannot be accessed—He becomes like an unused treatment intervention—useless. The victim has access to this untapped power of the Holy Spirit to lead the way. That is why

RECONCILIATION ADVISOR VS. THE PROFESSIONAL

in God's Word Jesus calls the Holy Spirit Whom He promises to give her, a "Helper."

A personal relationship with Christ via the Holy Spirit is different than following a book with a theological formula or being a part of a religious organization. In the proper context, theological books and religious affiliations are tools for growth; but it's not the same as the power of the work of the Holy Spirit Who can convert a victim into an *Overcomer*. There's no comparison with the victim's own strength to the unparalleled Holy Spirit guidance and energy the victim receives. Relying solely on her strength only leads to frustration, discouragement, and hopelessness—which can be alleviated by the reality of His Holy Presence. Realizing her need for and asking for the Holy Spirit's presence within her is the first step to receiving Christ's guidance.

For *some* people, the whole *idea* of being "born again" is very outlandish, but it's only outré to those who don't understand the things of God. Those who are unable to comprehend and discern spiritual things generally criticize and sometimes persecute believers (born again Christians). This reaction is not uncommon. Jesus was persecuted for being a believer as well—so much that He was hung on a cross for His belief in God the Father. It's not uncommon for unbelievers or bravado atheists to confront born-again Christians and say, "Well, if Jesus is alive, why don't you just have Him come back to Earth right now?" These nonbelievers have not read the gospel and God's plan for Jesus to return after *all* of His revelation has been completed. They don't comprehend the magnitude of His love for them, that He's even waiting for as many as will accept salvation so that none should perish! "The Lord is not slack concerning *His* promise, as some count slackness, but is longsuffering toward us, not willing that any should perish but that all should come to repentance" (2 Peter 3:9). God's Word says that He is *love* and He will keep His

Word and demonstrate that love even for nonbelievers; If God did not exist, we would not know or have *love*.

After you have instructed the victim on God's Word regarding the Holy Spirit, ask her if she's ready to be born again—to be born of the Spirit. Remind her that if she decides to be born of God, she will now have the Spirit of Christ Who dwells within her guiding her every step of the way in her journey to becoming an *Overcomer*. Make it clear to her that the Holy Spirit will convict her when she's headed on the wrong path; that the Spirit will teach her where she needs to grow. Let her know that if she decides to be born of God, from now on He will discipline her, encourage her, strengthen her, empower her, comfort her, and cover every facet of her life because of His unconditional love for her. This is all provided and sent to her through the Word of God (the Bible) and brothers- and sisters-in-Christ—and you, the professional.

How does a victim of abuse become born of God (Spiritually born again)? In the same way that any person in this world does: The instructions are found in the Word of God. To become born of God is the same as accepting Salvation (to be saved). God's Word tells us that in order to be born of God and have eternal life, we must repent of our sins and believe the Gospel, that Christ died for our sins, that He was buried, and that He rose again the third day after His death. Therefore, if she believes that Jesus (the only begotten Son of God) is the Christ our Savior Who died for our sins and was buried and rose for the forgiveness of our sins, then she has made her home in heaven by believing in Christ.

There is no day and time or place that's perfect to ask Christ into her heart. *Any* day, time, or place is right to accept Christ—God. All she needs to do is to feel led by the Spirit of God. Simply ask her if she's ready to ask Christ, the Holy Spirit, to dwell in her and to be saved.

RECONCILIATION ADVISOR VS. THE PROFESSIONAL

The Bible says that we are *all* sinners by inheritance; that we *need* to ask to be forgiven so as to reconcile and get right with God in order to be saved. "For all have sinned and fall short of the glory of God" (Romans 3:23). "That if you confess with your mouth the Lord Jesus and believe in your heart that God has raised Him from the dead, you will be saved. For with the heart one believes unto righteousness, and with the mouth confession is made unto salvation" (Romans 10:9-10).

If at some point the victim of abuse is ready to receive Christ (to be born of God), and if she declares that she would like to begin her journey as an *Overcomer* with her Heavenly Father as her Guide, she may want to pray something similar to this:

> "Father God, for reasons known to You, I am in need of Your forgiveness. I come to You today, asking for Your forgiveness for the life that I have lived and ask for Your forgiveness for_____.
> I believe that Your Son, Jesus Christ, died for my sins so that I could have eternal life. I now accept You, Jesus Christ, as my Lord and personal Savior, and I thank You for my gift of eternal life. Jesus, come into my heart; take charge, and transform me so that I may glorify and honor You with my life. I pray and ask for Your healing in the Name and power of Jesus, Amen."

If she prayed that prayer and asked to receive Christ in her life, encourage her to celebrate! Congratulate her and remind her that He's her new eternal friend! Implant within her heart that through the Holy Spirit, He's her new twenty-four-seven Companion for all of her days. Assign her to continue this new relationship with Christ daily and to get to know Him better through reading His Word, attending a Bible-teaching church, and developing relationships with other believers. Announce the good news to her that as she proceeds in her new knowledge of and life in Christ, she can be prepared to overcome her battle with abuse!

The Spirit, Mind, and Body
In the previous section, we discussed the Spirit. Let's now talk about the Mind and its connection to the Spirit. Our Spirit actually plays a big part in developing and shaping our mind. The Spirit helps the Mind to always take inventory of life situations and to explore not just one's will but also the wisdom as to how our decisions or choices affect ourselves and others in the present and future. Seeking God's help and His will for one's life—and His will for others—is a *mindfulness* decision. *Mindfulness* entails purposely paying attention to present experiences as they occur moment by moment without reacting with mindless thoughts or actions. *Mindless* thoughts or actions are symptoms of brokenness in the mind. Someone once said, "A broken bone doesn't heal on its own and neither does a broken mind."

The basic behavior of being actively *mindful* in all life activities is a power booster to the *neurotransmitters* in our brain. Something else to consider then, is our neurotransmitters. Neurotransmitters are chemical substances located and released in the brain. A neurotransmitter is produced and secreted by a neuron that then diffuses across a synapse, which causes excitation or inhibition of yet another neuron. A deficiency in these neurotransmitters can chemically imbalance our mood. (Neurotransmitters and mood affect are further discussed in this section on Balancing Your Body.)

Mindful behavior elevates our immune system and self-esteem, mediates our thoughts, moderates our appetite, regulates our stress levels, and develops our cognitive skills and peace of mind. This kind of *mindfulness* can ignite a human's awareness, which then enhances the sense of knowing and enables the person to further experience being fully awakened in the mind (fully alive), culminating in a new way of noticing details and obtaining a clarity and a sense of energy which then supports the person's Spirit, Mind, Body and overall social well-being.

Mindfulness-based practices are as ancient as *praying*. However, in the midst of modernization and technology, this type of mental activity is for some like a lost art. That is unfortunate because it is such a vital part in the treatment of the whole person. It's not an activity in which we have to stop what we're doing in order to perform such a meditative exercise; it's a natural, mental process that can become a daily part of our functioning. Research has concluded that *mindfulness* can improve a person's sense of well-being through improving concentration and flexibility. Regardless of outward circumstances, a person's practice of *mindfulness* is associated with learning to approach their challenging circumstances rather than withdrawing from them. The research interprets this as a sign of *neural resilience*. If a person is *willing* to practice *mindfulness* consistently, *mindfulness* can train the Mind, and it can become a way of being which shapes the ongoing neurological health of the person's life.

Let's move on and talk more deeply about the Mind and *why* it's so important for the victim to work on *how* her new *Overcomer* Mind can think and *why* developing the skill of *mindfulness* in all of her areas of her life becomes ever so relevant. *Mindfulness* is necessitous because a victim usually feels as if the abuser has stolen a portion of her *mind* and individual life on which she has missed out. Once free from the abuse, she will find that God is faithful, and she can retrieve her ability to use her *mind*, think on her own, and pick up her life where she left off. The victim's task if she is to become an *Overcomer* is to deprogram herself from all of the faulty thinking messages and actions that the abuser programmed into her mind and reprogram herself with the *truth* about her person so as to reconcile with herself.

Deprograming her Mind doesn't come naturally to a victim that has been living in the entrapment of an abusive relationship. At the beginning stages of entering into the *Overcomer* life, the victim may feel as if she's migrating into a new life that has an unknown culture, for she has been entrapped for so long in a culture of abuse. Once safely outside of the abuse, it's like she's a stranger in her own hometown since she has been in seclusion from the way the average person lives. This newfound freedom from control feels like she's enthralled, in a sense of wonder that a child has when participating in a new experience. The more time spent autonomously, the more re-oriented she will become with what is a healthy, wholesome way of living in relationships; she learns or re-learns what ordinary normalness is—her "new normal."

It is impossible for a victim's Mind (brain) to go unchanged if she decides to become an *Overcomer* because brain research has proven that we *can* change our brain neurologically with new life experiences. The victim's new experiences can facilitate brain changes into an *Overcomer* perspective. As an *Overcomer*, her new Mind (brain changes) allow her to have a new brain appraisal center whereby she can incorporate what's old in her abuse trauma life or eliminate it according to her new standards and goals for mental well-being.

Let's discuss how the Body interplays with the Spirit and Mind. A victim that balances her interactions between her Spirit and Mind is simply treating her body with respect. A healthy body is one that is not defiled by self-abuse or the abuse of others. It is a body that is well-nourished with natural foods as opposed to processed foods. A balanced body is stretched or exercised in between work and other activities; it is a body that develops a high immune system that is resistant to disease.

RECONCILIATION ADVISOR VS. THE PROFESSIONAL

It becomes relevant to discuss bodily care with victims who have suffered from the trauma of emotional and/or physical abuse to bring about copious awareness and to evaluate body health in the present; but, it is also important to review the after-effects that can infiltrate a victim's body as she ages. It's not only about the healed broken heart and bones; for example, if a victim has experienced attempted strangulation, this in and of itself can lead to later physical body concerns such as a stroke. There are numerous physical symptoms that can develop as a result of chronic stress during the crisis time span and/or in later years. Therefore, the best strategy is to inform the victim of the possibilities in order to prevent future illness and promote her healthy well-being.

The goal of the helper/professional is not to just provide guidelines to improve the functioning of the victim's body—her physical state—but to also equip her with knowledge about *how* the state of her Spirit and Mind affect the state of her Body. The best intervention is not to just offer information which will only serve as a temporary band-aid, but also to assign therapeutic homework assignments to be practiced daily so that they can become a lifestyle of *Overcomer* self-care! Most victims of abuse will immediately decide how difficult it sounds to focus on taking care of themselves, but reassure her that over time with education, practice, new habit-forming, and discipline, it is possible to rediscover the energy to take care of herself. She may initially not have the motivation to even care about herself, but the good news is that using energy begets gaining energy. So, begin with small, therapeutic self-care assignments with which she can have successes and grow into other self-care exercises which she can do one step at a time (Volume II Part I spells out the benefits to the Spirit and Mind when the victim takes care of her Body; it has several examples of self-care exercises in which the victim can engage to heal her body from the trauma of abuse, including a covenant which the victim signs to commit to taking care of her Spirit, Mind, and Body.)

Earlier in this section, I said that neurotransmitters would be discussed while discussing the Body. Neurotransmitters are important to discuss when treating a victim of abuse because this work involves both the emotional and physical symptoms of the abuse trauma. Menstruation, pregnancy, perimenopause, and menopause can *all* trigger emotional and physical responses. Hormonal imbalances can lead to psychological and physical reactions. Emotional and physiological responses (moods and physiological triggers) *can't* be controlled without balancing the brain and body chemistry. For example, there are three neurotransmitters that can quickly boost or drop your mood. *In order to control mood swings, it's highly important to balance the brain's neurotransmitters.* Some family physicians will not order lab tests for neurotransmitters and will often make a referral for the lab tests to be ordered by a psychiatrist.

The neurotransmitters worthy of evaluating when a victim of abuse is struggling with chronic stress and a mood disorder are *norepinephrine, serotonin,* and *dopamine. The following are the neurotransmitters that she can, with the proper steps, learn to balance*:

Norepinephrine—A deficiency in norepinephrine is closely associated with depression. Low levels of norepinephrine bring on lack of motivation, increased appetite, cravings for starchy foods, distractibility, difficulty starting or finishing tasks, feeling "blah" or gloomy, lethargic feelings, and ongoing fatigue. Norepinephrine helps a person pay attention and stay alert; it provides the ability to sustain concentration and focus.

Serotonin—Low levels of serotonin are also associated with anxiety and depression. A deficiency in serotonin can lead to insomnia, inability to relax, obsessive compulsive disorder, irrational behavior patterns, anxiety, panic attacks, irritability, moodiness, premenstrual syndrome, cravings for sweets or starchy foods, and/or eating disorders. Serotonin is known as the "feel happy" or "feel good" neurotransmitter. Generally, people with a serotonin deficiency seek activities or relationships that will nurture their need to feel good.

Dopamine—Dopamine is the neurotransmitter that handles anything to do with pleasure. A consistent deficiency in dopamine places the person at risk for becoming addicted to any source of pleasure (work, money, sex, cigarettes, alcohol, drugs, gambling, shopping, TV/media games, food, sleeping, and/or isolation). Chronic stress reduces dopamine. Low levels of dopamine bring on cravings for salty or fatty foods, mood swings, low tolerance for frustration, irritability, forgetfulness, and excessive sleeping. Most people with a dopamine deficiency can become apathetic, procrastinate, and don't have much enthusiasm for anything; they can become moody and depressed and seek pleasure in things to pacify their downcast feelings.

Low levels of *any* of the neurotransmitters in the victim's brain can have a major impact on how her Spirit, Mind, and Body function. Although a neurotransmitter deficiency does not always include symptoms of depression, too often victims of abuse trauma are prescribed antianxiety or antidepressant drugs to treat the symptoms of a neurotransmitter deficiency which has *not* been diagnosed. This is very counter-productive and ineffective for a victim or *Overcomer* because when the drugs prescribed do not work, their chronic stress increases and may even cause neurotransmitter levels to drop even lower. Testing neurotransmitter levels can get to the root of the neurochemical problem.

Eating nutritious meals, exercising, and taking neurotransmitter supplements combined with *mindful thinking* can be instrumental in treating a neurotransmitter imbalance. Antianxiety and antidepressant drugs have many side effects that only complicate the symptoms of a neurotransmitter deficiency. If the victim is experiencing any of the neurotransmitter deficiency symptoms that have been described, it would be to her benefit to be tested for a deficiency. If she wants to be tested (but prefers not to be tested through a local physician and lab), she can go on the internet and order a non-invasive urine lab test to check her neurotransmitter levels. She can go to: www.neurorelief.com. After she receives her test results, she should be encouraged to talk to her physician about the natural treatment options he/she would recommend.

Why does a professional want to discuss hormones in the middle of treating victim abuse trauma? Primarily because hormones evolve from our brain—the very important center of her well-being. For our brain to function adequately, it must have balanced hormonal levels. Women of all ages can experience hormonal deficiencies, *especially* those undergoing chronic stress. A woman's functioning and well-being can be influenced by hormonal imbalances. For example, the female hormone *estrogen* helps to balance the neurotransmitters in the brain. It also aids in regulating or maintaining the following bodily functions: blood sugar levels, sleep, metabolic rate, muscle mass, memory, appetite, mood, weight, osteoporosis prevention, and premenstrual, menstrual, and menopausal symptom regulation.

Communicate to the victim that the path to reaching her *Overcomer* goals begins by balancing her Spirit, Mind, and Body and that the time to start taking care of them is *now*. Point out to her that the very reason that she took the step to seek help from you *is* reason enough to believe that *she is ready* to make healthy choices and changes in her abusive lifestyle. Taking care of her Spirit, Mind, and Body will provide her with the gift of a balanced mental health, which can bring self-confidence, hope, and *peace*. Bring to her awareness that her life as a victim is a life of unpredictable danger; taking care of her Spirit, Mind, and

RECONCILIATION ADVISOR VS. THE PROFESSIONAL

Body can give her the assurance of a healthy balanced lifestyle as an *Overcomer*. Help her to focus on and to make a commitment to a balanced Spirit, Mind, and Body. Because if her *mindset* is strictly on her abusive relationship and she ignores her Spirit, Mind, and Body, then whatever she focuses on the *most* is what she and her life will become. Following the strategies for balancing the Spirit, Mind, and Body will ensure that the victim—soon to become *Overcomer*—will maximize her therapeutic effects.

God decided thousands of years ago that no one ever reaches a stage in life where one cannot start over. Your duty is to convey to the victim that God is a God of compassion and grace Who can make her and everything around new—because every dawn to God is a new beginning. "*Through* the LORD's mercies we are not consumed, Because His compassions fail not. *They are* new every morning; Great *is* Your faithfulness" (Lamentations 3:22-23). Let the victim know that if she truly wants to make a fresh start that all she needs to do is make a firm decision to end her past life of abuse (even though that life attempts to enslave her). Reiterate to her that a new life can come from God. Continually affirm to her that if she asks God for that new life of peace, she will receive it because it is the inheritance of a new life that is by grace hers through Christ. Leave her heart sealed with the truth that God is a God of love, startups, and start overs!

How Can a Victim Become an *Overcomer*?
Before we can discuss how a victim can become an *Overcomer*, it's important to review what an *Overcomer* is. I have always elected not to use the term "survivor" when referring to any victim that has recovered from abuse. The reason for not using the term "survivor" is because I don't believe in working with victims just to help them exist; I want to encourage them to *stop* living a life of abuse—to permanently conquer and have victory over abuse! As previously mentioned, definitions of *survivor* cite

the meaning as "to remain alive or in existence, live on." The synonyms suggested for *survive* are "ride out, weather, and make it through." A victim doesn't just want to weather and ride out her abuse or make it through her trauma—she wants a permanent resolution to her abuse.

When I set goals with victims, or when I refer to those that have recovered from their abuse, I have always used the term "*Overcomer*." Definitions and the meaning of "overcome" include "to defeat; conquer, to prevail over, surmount, be victorious." Some synonyms for *overcome* are "stop, triumph." Moreover, in addition to the definitions and the meaning of an *Overcomer* are the biblical descriptions that define an "*Overcomer*," which are also more fitting to the quest of a victim who seeks peace and a permanent recovery from her abusive past, present, and future.

The biblical definitions of *Overcomer* are filled with *hope* and *promises for restoration* and *peace*. A victim does not have *hope*—an *Overcomer* does. The definition of *hope* includes the happiness and the good to look forward to. The word *hope* comes from the Greek word *elpis*, which means to anticipate with pleasure, expectation, or confidence. An *Overcomer* can rest securely in her future because she has *hope*. Furthermore, the biblical definitions of *Overcomer* address the conjoint realms of the victim's Spirit, Mind, and Body, which, when balanced, produce *peace*.

The Bible equips us with examples of how we are to live our lives. It instructs us on *how* to rise above our circumstances—in order to live victoriously as *Overcomers*. Followers of Christ are called various names, which include *believers, little children, Christians, and Overcomers*. The victim discovers that she is invited to have an indivisible union with Christ Himself, and as a result, she can *become* a partaker of His victorious, divine nature, which includes the reality that He has power—*He is* an *Overcomer!* An *Overcomer* has the power in Christ to thrive, not just survive.

RECONCILIATION ADVISOR VS. THE PROFESSIONAL

> "These things I have spoken to you, that in Me you may have peace. In the world you will have tribulation; but be of good cheer, I have overcome the world" (John 16:33).

Christ is not only offering the victim to partake in His divinity (Spirit) and everything that Christ represents (His character), but since He *is* a victor, He's also offering an opportunity for her to partake in His victory as an *Overcomer*. Anyone who is of God *is* an *Overcomer*! The victim is given an option to accept and receive *all* of Christ's inheritance once born of God (See Part IV for the definition of being born of God.).

> "For whatever is born of God overcomes the world. And this is the victory that has overcome the world—our faith" (1 John 5:4).

> "You are of God, little children, and have overcome them, because He who is in you is greater than he who is in the world" (1 John 4:4).

It is *Christ* Who calls the victim to become an *Overcomer*, just like Christ calls each one of us to overcome any of our circumstances. An *Overcomer* is promised that she can overcome her troubles with Earth, satan, and hell. Once she accepts Christ and His salvation, she's offered the joy of living with Christ in her heart and eternal life with Christ in heaven—to be in God's presence forever. Why does Christ call her to overcome her abuse? Because He does not want her to remain trapped in an abusive relationship—His desire is for her highest good! Christ's desire for the victim is justice and peace of mind. Access to justice and peace: Christ.

A victim who has endured the vicious cycle of the trauma of abuse and has reached her lowest point of despair is ready to make a decision to *overcome* her abuse because her daily abusive living is so unbearable; it overpowers her. She is set to reprogram her victim thoughts into *Overcomer* mindfulness. She is at a peak significant growth point. This stage, although an entrance into the light of freedom from abuse, is a most vulnerable and pressurized state. This is when, regardless of limited or no support from others and even while too despondent to know what to pray for, she turns all her pain, fears, and concerns over to Christ Who is all too aware of what she's been through. The One Who is her refuge and strength and ever-present help in trouble *is* the very One she needs to turn to as her *Overcomer* Guide. The steps that a victim takes to become an *Overcomer* are as follow:

(1) *Die to self.* She has to die to her *old self* as a person and to separate herself from and give up the world she has been living in. It means to give up her personal, worldly plans for her life and to commit to solely living for Christ. Paul speaks about his dying of the self in the Bible:

> 'I have been crucified with Christ; it is no longer I who live, but Christ lives in me; and the *life* which I now live in the flesh I live by faith in the Son of God, who loved me and gave Himself for me" (Galatians 2:20).

When a victim surrenders her life to Christ, she is enraptured by His love; her entire perspective on life changes. She is able to envision *overcoming* her abuse through His love as He becomes her strength, shield, *hope* and her *peace*.

(2) *Love Christ.* God's Word encourages her to love Him back as *He first* loved her. The victim now realizes that without loving Christ, it is *impossible* to overcome anything. A victim learns that accepting Christ's love causes a movement within her and others. An *Overcomer* dwells in the Spirit of Christ's love—the Spirit of *change*.

> "We love Him because He first loved us" (1 John 4:19).

> "You shall love the Lord your God with all your heart, with all your soul, and with all your mind" (Matthew 22:37).

> "But He said, 'The things which are impossible with men are possible with God'" (Luke 18:27).

(3) Believe that Jesus is the Christ. An *Overcomer* must *believe* that Christ *is* our Savior, her Redeemer, and *Truth*. She must not have an intellectual understanding of Christ; she must have a surrendered acceptance of the meaning of being born of God and of *Who* Jesus Christ *is*. She must *believe* that Christ *is* who He says He *is*. The foundation of an *Overcomer* is that she *believes* in Christ. She must believe in faith with Christ's faith—the kind of faith that *overcomes* the world! An *Overcomer* has to believe that Jesus *is* God in three persons and that He was crucified by sinners (us) and died for our sins. Surrendering can only be done by those who are born of God, *believe*, and want to be *Overcomers*. When an *Overcomer believes* and *trusts* God, she experiences the power of the Holy Spirit's properties which Christ longs to give her.

> "And the Father Himself, who sent Me, has testified of Me. You have neither heard His voice at any time, nor seen His form. But you do not have

His word abiding in you, because whom He sent, Him you do not believe" (John 5:37-38).

"That if you confess with your mouth the Lord Jesus and believe in your heart that God has raised Him from the dead, you will be saved" (Romans 10:9).

(4) *Christ comes first.* To become an *Overcomer* means Christ the Lord must come first—not the world. An *Overcomer* looks daily toward the highest power first—Christ. Being an *Overcomer* is an *everyday* lifetime commitment. By approaching God's throne daily and making Him her first priority, the victim is transformed into the likeness of Christ. To become Christ-like, she has to spend daily time in His Word so that she may have victory over temptations, tribulations, and endure the world—like Christ has—*as an Overcomer*!

"And do not be conformed to this world, but be transformed by the renewing of your mind, that you may prove what *is* that good and acceptable and perfect will of God" (Romans 12:2).

"For whom He foreknew, He also predestined *to be* conformed to the image of His Son" (Romans 8:29).

An *Overcomer* has principles that she abides by; she remains true to her principles, does not suppress her *Overcomer* ideals, and does not bow to the societal pressures to remain a victim. An *Overcomer*'s principles include mindfully balancing her Spirit, Mind, and Body.

RECONCILIATION ADVISOR VS. THE PROFESSIONAL

To become an *Overcomer* means to disown the victim mentality. When she gives up her victim role, God reveals His purpose for her. The victim learns that to become an *Overcomer* is not an unreachable, pious dream; through Christ and the Holy Spirit's help, it is an obtainable goal! The result of surrendering her victim role is the purge of her brokenness; she does this by letting go of her self-will and emerging into being transformed as an *Overcomer*. Becoming an *Overcomer* is a choice with a positive outcome. The outcome is living a life of peace because the sublime peace of Christ *is* the foundation of an *Overcomer*'s life.

When a victim chooses to be an *Overcomer*, her future readily unfolds before her with all its promises from God—His thoughts and plans for a hopeful future with a life of goodness and peace are set in motion just as soon as she seeks and calls upon Him! "For I know the thoughts that I think toward you, says the Lord, thoughts of peace and not of evil, to give you a future and a hope. Then you will call upon Me and go and pray to Me, and I will listen to you. And you will seek Me and find *Me,* when you search for Me with all your heart" (Jeremiah 29:11-13). There is no ideal day for a victim to leave her victim role and to become an *Overcomer*—today is always that day! For a victim, choosing an *Overcomer* life is a purposeful resolve, or it does not happen. An *Overcomer*, contrary to a victim, *consistently operates her lifestyle from the lens of God*. An *Overcomer* maintains an attitude of peaceful confidence and faces the future with expectation. You as a victim's helper can encourage a victim to choose her future wisely—to choose to become an *Overcomer*!

Helping to Heal & Stop the Trauma of Victim Abuse
Having been a victim of abuse is like having lived through a war because abuse leaves the aftermath like the destruction of war. Abuse attacks women and their children, destroying their identity, invading their freedom, stagnating their social, emotional,

economic, spiritual, and physical growth, instilling fear, breaking their hearts, reducing emotional confidence, wounding and scarring, humiliating, splitting family and mother-child relationships, inducing fear and guilt, severing trust between strangers, friends, and family, and causing them to live deceived, resentfully, with overwhelming confusion, and anxiety. Some victim's war and war aftermath affects their loved ones who have had to stand back and watch the victim suffer. The good news is that no one has to stand back or be on the sidelines of this abuse war; anyone can choose to become an advocate by saying "no" to abuse so that it doesn't continue to infect our society—our nation.

Through the pages of this book, I have advocated for abused women by educating them on the steps to take to *recognize* what is happening to them—*abuse*. I have provided information to encourage the victim to seek help for her protection for the sake of her safety and that of her children. Along with this message, I have encouraged the victim to become a pacesetter in not only pursuing her own healing, but also in becoming compelled to propel this quest to heal unto other victims of abuse. She absolutely cannot deal with the aftermath of the destruction of abuse without *first* becoming an *Overcomer*. The abuser is not only a danger to victims, but he also sets a pace for an endangered society. With your help and the assistance of communities and society, together you and I *and Overcomers* can then proceed to advocate for a non-abusive, tolerant nation. We were each created and born from God. We are a part of God's eternal agenda; God uses us in His supernatural enterprises to do God's work for the world.

I will summarize a review at this time as to *what* the victim must accomplish in order to succeed in becoming an *Overcomer* and prospect for advocating for victims. As has been discussed, an abuser attempts to destroy the mind and life of his victim

RECONCILIATION ADVISOR VS. THE PROFESSIONAL

so that her life becomes his. The primary path for the victim's healing, therefore, is to deprogram herself out of the abuser's indoctrination and redirect her thinking back to devoting herself to using *her own thinking* and the taking care of herself and her children. Her main focus as a victim is to *stop* investing her Spirit, Mind, and Body on the abuser and redirect her focus toward moving out of the war zone, moving on with her life, moving forward in spite of the aftermath of war and following *her own course* as an *Overcomer*. With your help (as the *Overcomer* becomes ready), she can ultimately begin to take additional action against her victimization, which, in turn, can continue to empower her. This does not mean that she is to convert herself into an activist for victims of abuse, but it simply means living her life as an *Overcomer* and finding that speaking out about anti-victimization at the right time and place is of great help to anyone that is being victimized. It is *her cue* and to her advantage to use her new voice as an *Overcomer*—for silence condones and implies an acceptance of abuse and victimization.

This book has given an overview of our historical beginnings of abuse in our society which have created an acceptance and condoning of family abuse, casting the responsibility on the victims. One person at a time in our society can influence the future of our culture's historical excusing of oppression and victimization of women and children. Our nation's population can stand up and say, "Any type of abuse is a crime"—period. Centuries back, the courts acknowledged the right of husbands to beat their wives; what if courts across our nation were to acknowledge the abuse of women and children as criminal conduct?! The current statutes allow abusers to leave the courtroom with minimal or no consequences; therefore, women and children are set up for re-victimization. When the act of abuse is charged with the punishment of a lesser offense, such as with a traffic violation, instead of a misdemeanor or a felony in criminal law, it enables repeat offenses.

In the 1990s, the public's outrage over family violence resulted in domestic abuse being included in the Violent Crime Control and Law Enforcement Act of 1994. Through the Title IV, Violence Against Women Act (VAWA), domestic violence and sexual assault research and educational programs were authorized for judges and judicial staff. It provided funds for shelters and police training, enhanced victim privacy and protection, and increased penalties for domestic violence and rape. In 2000, the U.S. Supreme Court declared part of this Act as unconstitutional. In particular, it was decided that if Congress could federalize domestic assault and rape, then it was difficult to rule out anything that it couldn't. The recommendation was made that "gender-motivated" violence and sexual assault should be combated without making a federal case of it. This legal reasoning only endorses the pervasive, condoning attitude in the U.S. judicial system and our society: that family violence is a "domestic" issue and not the crime of an abuser against a woman or child.

The prohibition and punishment of any act of family violence can only protect the welfare and safety of our society—there's no reason why state legislature cannot make *any type of abuse* criminally illegal. With the exception of the emotional abuse of "infidelity" which God the Supreme Judge has already ruled as against His Commandments (law) "You shall not commit adultery" (Exodus 20:14), there are no laws against *emotional abuse*. Justice can only happen for a victim attacked by multiple types of abuse, if there are laws against *all* abuse. Justice seems impossible only when it is looked upon as a lofty ideal. If a nation stands in agreement and puts the responsibility on its people to *change* the enabling of abusers, the results are a culture that accepts that women and children are to be deeply respected and protected.

RECONCILIATION ADVISOR VS. THE PROFESSIONAL

This renewed cultural attitude ought to follow suit from the government down to its people, through literature, the educational system, media messages, and domestic violence programs within every corporation/business establishment/organization. It is our culture that drives abuse to remain the way that it is. Victims do make choices about themselves and their abuse parallel to the path of prior social upbringing and/or based on society's attitude toward spousal abuse, choices that are pivotal in their tolerance and participation in the abuse. These choices lead the victim further into the pit of trauma and despair, but they are at the time the best safety choices a victim can make, given how informed she is about abuse and the milieu in her society.

There is no legitimate excuse for refusing to solve the problem of abuse in our society. It is those who ally with the abuser who are the ones that don't see abuse as a solvable problem. In some smaller towns or upscale neighborhoods, families, neighbors, and friends alike are reluctant to admit to spousal abuse and family violence among the people they know personally. Many community members will actually ask themselves: what did the victim do to make the abuser angry? A highly regarded abuser is seen as a *civil individual,* and it's easier for community members to assume that his attack on the victim was just a blunder and fumble. There are those that are more worried about being politically correct than the safety of a victim and her children. Some people in our society have become lazy, apathetic, unconcerned, or are discouraged with a belief that abuse is just a part of life.

Some people are afraid to stand up to the problem of abuse; these folks are allowing the abuser to *silence them* as he has done with his victim(s). There's a myth that society and even those in the helping professions tend to believe—that abuse inflicted by a loved one is not as bad as stranger abuse. There's a variation from state to state and court to court, but generally the pattern has been that *abuse* is not prosecuted, and it is seen as less serious than other crimes. It is not uncommon for violence in the home to be overlooked in comparison to stranger assault and for the victim to back off from reporting her marital abuse because she is not taken seriously. "Research shows that we interpret violence perpetrated by strangers differently from violence that intimates inflict."[7] "Indeed, female victims of domestic violence are six times less likely to report the crime to the police or other officials than those who have suffered at the hands of a stranger."[8]

A victim that is cautious about or even petrified of reporting her marital abuse *or* those that are fearfully advocating for victims of abuse trauma *must* be encouraged to reconsider their position. Our society has to be made aware of abuse myths and educated on the fact that abuse affects *all of us,* even if we're not directly involved in family violence. Our communities must be informed that if each one of us stands up against family violence, our quality of life in our society can be recovered through the restitution of the family as it was created to be—non-abusive. It is *only* when law enforcement, the judicial system, clergy, educators, physicians, and clinicians *voice* their sensitivity to the complex quagmire of spousal and family abuse that victims' and their children's lives are saved. Benjamin Franklin's insight that "an ounce of prevention is worth a pound of cure" reminds us that the first line of defense to problem-solving *is* prevention. How do we prevent spousal and family abuse from happening in our society? As has been presented in this book, the victim *must* be educated about the dynamics of abuse and transition *must* take place from her victim role into an *Overcomer* of abuse. Professionals (physicians, therapists, law enforcement, judicial systems, clergy, and laypersons) must receive training on the trauma of abuse. Annual family violence conferences must be held for professionals and first responders in *every* state of our

RECONCILIATION ADVISOR VS. THE PROFESSIONAL

nation. However, society must also do their part locally in educating the state and communities about abuse.

Some states have a Governor's Commission for Women. Prevention of spousal and family violence could be assisted if *all* states would maintain *active* commissions for women. The purpose of such a commission is to promote the quality of life and status of women. The commission's role is to advise the governor and the legislature on the needs of women in their community by identifying problems and recommending policies and procedures in the areas of family, workplace, violence, and equity of women's participation in society. Some commissions have been known to create resource brochures for victims and abusers. On the other hand, some states have only produced resource brochures for teen dating abuse, skipping family violence. More work has to be done in making resource information readily available to victims of spousal and family abuse. It is *not* just about raising public awareness through occasional media programs or temporary family violence educational campaigns. Prevention of spousal and family abuse by every state means addressing the problem not on a surface or activist level but starting with including abuse awareness and prevention education as part of the required school educational curriculums. In addition, all colleges and universities must require that educators and other professionals be trained on abuser and victim dynamics and certified in family abuse trauma. Furthermore, professionals need to be instructed on how to train lay people on the identification, prevention, and assistance with the dynamics of abuse.

Educators have done great work in preventing sexual abuse through teaching preschool children about *good touch* and *bad touch,* but somehow, they have ignored spousal and family violence. Just as the way that they have created sensitive and appropriate programs to teach preschool and elementary school children about sexual abuse, and just as the way that they have been teaching middle and high school students about date rape, prevention of family violence can similarly be taught. If school systems incorporate teaching boys and girls the difference between healthy, functional relationships and abusive relationships, our society can prevent the acceptance of family abuse. Schools do not just teach academics; they also role model and improve social skills. A wall of legislators against family violence is necessary. Once the government supports educational systems to recognize and participate in the teaching of family violence awareness and prevention, it will become a natural part of the school system's lexicon *as if* this is a part of teaching social skills!

Perhaps educators, professionals, and lay persons in the community may voice that they feel as if they are intruding or crossing the line when they validate spousal abuse at school or in society, but it is this validation that stops the silence and the blaming of the victim(s). Your response should not be one of feeling like you're imposing but one of a protective society that is outraged by family violence. When family violence education or assistance is offered to a victim and her family, she experiences vindication. This gives her a hope, a chance to become abuse-free. It helps her to realize that neither she nor the children are responsible for the family violence; your external voices help the victim set her family free from abuse in the present and for generations to come. Health.com compiled a list of the "10 Worst States for Women's Health" from the Kaiser Family Foundation, the National Women's Law Institute, and the Guttmacher Institute data. The indicators of women's health focused on physical healthcare screenings, poverty, and maternal mortality rates. In this report, a member of the House of Representatives is quoted in 2011 as stating that she is "very cognizant" that women are suffering *but* that "common sense legislation that could really improve the lot of women doesn't even get out of committee here."

RECONCILIATION ADVISOR VS. THE PROFESSIONAL

The resolution of domestic violent crimes is influenced by individual choices, our socialization process, our cultural environment, research, healthcare, *and* public policy. A comprehensive approach to studying, preventing, and resolving the problem of victim and family violence in our nation *must* take place; it *cannot* be left behind at "committee level." If our states and communities are informed about the towering statistics of domestic violent crimes, then they can make it a priority healthcare problem, and they can get involved to influence state policies and transform our state health systems to include the prevention of family violence as a healthcare goal! Our nation's health can then, and only then, be realistically examined to know what works and doesn't work in dealing with domestic violence and to use what's just, what works, and what is promising in the prevention of domestic crimes. As an *informed* society, the perception of marital abuse that the wider world has can change. Abused wives are invisible through their silence, and our nation doesn't comprehend how life-altering being a victim of the trauma of abuse can be. If they understood this, the social support would be made available.

Professionals may feel like they play the heavy in having to legitimize spousal and family abuse. In addition to the victim getting out of the denial state of abuse, professionals themselves must acknowledge the phenomenon of spousal abuse—and *break the silence* in society. The act of abuse and victimization will not stop until our society stops making excuses for abusers, their friends, and families that perpetrate! The current progress in society's or the abuser's work to decrease family violence is stalled. We must come together as professionals and as a society with a national campaign to penalize *any type of abuse* as a criminal act.

We will not have an abuse-free society unless the perpetrator (the abuser) is confronted and firmly told that *he is* the number one problem in our nation's family violence statistics. The abuser will not be held accountable until our society demands his accountability for his abusive crimes against his victim(s). *If* the victim's silence is broken and all of the other voices (lay people, professionals, legal system, family and friends, the government) are *consistently* activated and heard, it can be a powerful societal reinforcement that the only responsible party for the abuse is the abuser. *Every* healthy approach to the healing of abuse begins with *breaking the silence*! The key then is for our nation to allow victims and our society to *refrain from silence*, renounce it, and to place the responsibility of abuse as the established punishable crime of the abuser.

> **"Then they cried out to the Lord in their trouble,**
> *And* **He saved them out of their distresses. He sent His word and healed them,**
> **And delivered** *them* **from their destructions."**
>
> - Psalm 107:19-20 -

HANNAH'S STORY

MY HUSBAND, JOE, AND I met in the middle of the U.S.A. I lived in the country, and he lived in a small town about ten miles from me. We went to the same school from sixth grade on up to our high school graduations. We were in band together and involved in other school activities. Joe was a year older than me, and he initially dated my sister. However, during my freshman year in college, my sister fell in love with one of Joe's classmates. It was *then* that she decided to set me up on a date with Joe. Joe and I dated, and we married my sophomore year of college. My sister and I always said Mother *loved* Joe; one of us had to marry him! Joe and I were both of the Protestant faith, and we had a church wedding. I accepted Christ as a child when I was six years old, but I wasn't certain when Joe had become a Christian; I just knew he had accepted Christ and had been baptized by middle school.

While we were in college, Joe dropped out his first year. Joe's family had a hardship that impacted the financing of his college tuition. I had a four-year scholarship, so I continued to attend and graduated with a degree in pediatric nursing. Joe took a position with a construction company. My plan was that once I graduated, I could work and put Joe through college to complete his degree. Joe decided not to return to college and instead attended a technology school, which landed him an excellent job in a corporation. Joe did very well as he climbed up the corporate ladder. I have two adult sons from my marriage to Joe. However, our marital problems began within the first three months of our marriage. Our living room was right next to our bedroom. Joe presumed that I was asleep in our bedroom. I saw a dim TV light on, but heard no volume in the living room, so I went in to turn it off. I walked in on Joe having sexual relations with a man on the couch.

Prior to this encounter, Joe had been the most loving husband; he's the first man *I* had ever been intimate with. We weren't having *any* marital sexual problems that I was aware of; we had sexual relations frequently. The only time that I could ever recall any sexual incompatibility between us was when he suggested activities that I was uncomfortable with, but he never complained about that. My heart was devastated. I was hurt *so deeply*; I didn't know I could hurt that bad. When I confronted Joe about what I had seen that night on the couch, he *emphatically denied* it and dismissed any responsibility or immorality on his behalf (he believed in what made you feel good). Joe would openly ask me if I would be interested in swinging partners. Once, he brought home a young co-worker who was fond of me and said that *if I* was interested in him, it was fine with him—for *me* to have relations with *him*! I, of course, said, "Over my dead body!"

I tried very hard after I caught him with that first bisexual extramarital affair to capture his interest in *me*. I would make myself attractive for him, even to the extent of buying sexy negligées for our intimate times. But nothing seemed to work. I was being mistreated. This was alien to me, as I didn't grow up being mistreated, and neither did he. Joe came from a loving

HANNAH'S STORY

two-parent family, and I was raised by my wonderful, widowed mother. The only thing that I could figure out is that Joe may have been sexually abused as a teen by a man in town. There was a man in his community that was known for buying liquor for the young men in our high school, and he would have boys over to his home. This is the same man that was on the couch with Joe that night in our home. It was common knowledge that some of the boys that were this man's visitors had become practicing bisexuals or homosexuals; some of them were even diagnosed HIV-positive later on.

Joe continued to deny his bisexuality whenever I suspected his activity with males. I was feeling *humiliated* and *confused* by his unaccountability with time, and our substantial incomes never seemed to make ends meet. Joe acted like my income was to support us and his income was just spending money; he usually just bought whatever he desired. I remember one time when he wanted a motorbike and he finally talked me into going to the store to buy it with him. That day, as we left the store, he went back into the store and asked that I stay in the car. Joe came back out with yet another motorbike—which he insisted was for me! We got into a financial bind, and our debt had become unmanageable. Whenever I inquired about our unexplainable, excessive debt, his resolve was that we would work it out. I repeatedly reminded him that we both had jobs and that we must pay off our bills!

I believe that tolerating, watching our children suffer, and an incident that Joe was involved in was the last straw for me. It was on a Friday night. Joe and I had a movie date to watch my favorite movie. It was our end of the week *fun time* as we both worked such long, hard hours all week. Joe didn't come home. Instead, I got a call from him later that evening asking me to please come and pick him up (he had gotten beat up). Apparently, he had stopped at a gay pick-up park after work, had been attacked, and left wearing only his necktie and socks. Joe had left his wedding ring in his car's glove compartment, and it was stolen by his attackers. This was the breaking point of our ten-year marriage. I couldn't deny his mistreatment of me *anymore,* and he couldn't deny his actions anymore. I feared for my life and my children's lives as his attackers kept calling our home, threatening that they would kill us if Joe pressed charges. Joe did press charges against his attackers.

I turned to my sister for support; she helped me to secure an attorney and to protectively hide my children from Joe's attackers. Between my sister's and mother's homes (which were an hour away from town), we were on hideout! I called on my pastor, and he graciously met me at the hospital where I worked; my church was of great support to me throughout this process. The church never knew why I had gotten a divorce; they just knew I had become a single parent. I asked my attorney to file for a separation because I didn't believe in divorce, but after I told him my marital story, he encouraged my sister to assist me in considering a divorce. I got my mother's sorrowful blessing on the divorce. Joe insisted that he did not want a divorce, which was very degrading to me as I knew he had been sexually active with multiple males and had even been living with one on and off in the past three years. The divorce was finalized; Joe's child support order was a meager amount because he claimed financial hardship. I ended up paying off all of our debt through my income—as well as *all* of the divorce legal fees.

Ten years after the divorce, I sought family counseling as I saw that our family was in disarray. I had noted that our oldest son was struggling in school, and the youngest wanted his father to admit to his own parents and my mother that he was living a bisexual lifestyle. I believe that Joe's past living of this dual lifestyle, my staying in the marriage with him, and a second marriage that wasn't working out led to our children being referred to an inpatient residential treatment facility.

During a counseling session in residential care, my oldest son declared that *he* was homosexual. I was not surprised as I had suspected that Joe had introduced him to his male companions. I myself had noticed Joe touch my son inappropriately on one occasion when my son had laid on the couch. I also thought back on my intuition, and suspicion, that most likely Joe had groomed my son *from birth* to become homosexual. I had often wondered if during diaper changes (because of what I saw after the diaper changes) if Joe was molesting him; but I never confronted Joe on the matter.

My second abusive marriage was to Jay. I had been divorced from Joe for three years when I remarried. Jay had been previously married and had custody of his two children. We met on a blind date that was set up by a co-worker who thought I would be a good match for him. My thinking was that if I didn't like him, I could certainly set him up with one of the many singles in my Christian singles group. Jay wasn't a Christian, and I thought perhaps at best I could lead him to a Christian environment at church and expose him to some Christian relationships. In the meantime, I had given some thought to the fact that he and I were unequally yoked. This was already being observed by my next-door neighbor who happened to be a pastor (he was concerned and warned me about dating someone who was not a person of faith). Shortly after that, Jay and I attended a singles Bible study. A friend who knew me as an active leader in my Christian singles ministry saw me with him at the Bible study. The very next day, she stopped by at my job to strongly caution me *not to* involve myself romantically with a non-believer. My friend actually said that she was uncertain if this was a safe or acceptable relationship for me—personally. She stipulated that I was a Christian and Jay wasn't and that he had a background that

I needed to take fully into consideration before continuing in a relationship with him.

I had rationalized to myself that if I didn't marry him, he was not going to leave me alone because I had already told him "no" once. I told him that I would give my right arm for him to become a Christian and that I *couldn't* marry him because we were unequally yoked. As it turned out, saying *no* to him was like waving a red flag in front of a bull. Jay *pursued* me *even more then*—amazingly! Also, I had unbelievable guilt as a Sunday school teacher and ministerial leader for having had pre-marital relations with him; I just felt that I *had to* marry him at that point. It was as if I had already mentally married him by going to bed with him. I had been sinful, and I didn't know how it could get any worse; of course, I found out *later* how it could get worse! I told myself that hopefully he would come to know Christ at some point in his life. I backed off spiritually because I decided I would rather he accept Christ on his own, not to do it deceitfully or forcefully (in order to marry me).

During the time that many were advising me against this marriage, one of my co-workers hired someone covertly to take me out on a date—in order to distract me from Jay. I had direction from pastors and many friends that said I needed to move on. I ignored all of the precautions, and Jay and I were engaged within five months of meeting and married within seven months of courtship! I didn't ask the pastor of my own church to marry us because deep inside, I knew it was wrong to marry a non-believer, so I asked a pastor from another church to marry us. I felt all the way up to Jay's proposal that he loved me more than anyone had ever loved me and that he treated me like gold! Jay seemed to just understand and know everything that I needed from my mind to my body. It was as if Jay read me like a book from our very first date. Even though Jay was not raised in a Christian home, he was a *good person* and came from a *good family*. However, he was not about to become a Christian, even when I took him with me to *all* of my Christian functions. Every time he went, he would shake during the invitational prayer—but that's as far as it went with him.

As I look back at our dating days, I believe that I was quite taken and overwhelmed by Jay's gentleman ways with me. I sensed a power within that had been taken away from me in my first marriage (because I had never attempted to take control of that marriage). I now believed that Jay loved me so much more than even I loved him. Before I became intimate with Jay, he was always very appropriate and well-mannered. My thoughts were, "Oh my goodness, this is a *real man* who *really* knows me as a woman; he has the ability to know my need for respect." Perhaps, I was also taken by the fact that he was attracted to me. This loving attention came to a gradual halt within the first year and a half of our marriage. All of his manipulative, loving attentions became clear to me during a time that I had to have surgery, and he left me in the care of our elementary school-age children to go golfing!

As time went by, I found myself financially abused by Jay. Even though he had a good job with the government, I discovered that he had been emptying out our income funds, including our savings, running up our credit cards. Our house was going to be repossessed, and Jay was planning to file bankruptcy! My response to his plan was one of outrage, and I declared that as a Christian, I would always be determined to pay my bills, and bankruptcy was not an option in my book! Come to find out, Jay had a problem with managing our resources; his philosophy was that if he wanted something, he was *entitled to it,* and he would just buy it, regardless of my opinion and whether we had the finances or not. Jay acted prideful, egotistical, selfish, and like a spoiled child whenever he couldn't have something.

It seemed like he couldn't handle it if he didn't have the money to buy something. It was then that it began to dawn on me that I made three times the income of his ex-wife; perhaps he saw me as a goldmine when he met me? One time he justified our buying of a new sports car so that we could donate *our car* to someone in need of a vehicle. I have reasons to believe that it was someone with whom he was having an extramarital affair with. Our relationship during this time (while I felt he was financially taking advantage of me) was still intimate, but as time progressed, he became distracted with other interests.

Jay had become disenchanted with his work due to missing out on several promotions, which he always blamed on other reasons but him. I later found out at his job what the *real reasons* were. Jay lost his job, but he didn't tell me for about two weeks (he left every day as if he was going to work). Jay did this until there was no money coming in on his behalf, and then he had to tell me. But even when he told me, he wouldn't tell me *why* they fired him; he would just say it was terribly unfair. I became suspicious of an affair because when he lost his job, a female employee in his office was let go at the same time; she called our home a couple of times after that.

Our marriage deteriorated as a result of Jay's irresponsible behavior with our relationship and finances, his son's abuse toward me, and our increasing discord resulting from his daughter having been sexually abused prior to our marriage. Jay's son was combative toward me; he *never* made the blended family adjustment (unlike his sister, who was proud to have me as her stepmom). Jay's son would yell out that he *hated me* and wanted his *real* mother. My stepson became *physically abusive* toward me. This, of course, created chaos with my attempts to raise my own two sons. I pursued family counseling, which Jay refused to attend. I believe he was concerned about having to self-disclose the financial issues he had gotten us into, and he was evading a discussion on his extramarital affairs that I had suspected.

When Jay refused to attend family counseling, the therapist recommended that I should change the home dynamics simply by never being left alone with my stepson who had bruised me. Jay was infuriated by this and balked at having to take his son everywhere with him (especially to his personal recreational activities). Or, at least that was what he complained about. I really don't know *where* Jay went at times; he could have been gambling instead of golfing or having an affair—for all I knew. I caught him in *so many lies* to me and my children—that I never knew what the truth was. Jay's ex-wife cheated on him, so I wouldn't be surprised if Jay was feeling as if he could do the same. I have wondered if his urgency to go golfing when I had my surgery was truly related to golf or his relationship with a couple of single women that were in our golf league. I had noticed that he had been especially friendly toward them. I do know that he was angry because his son tagging along cramped his style of being a *free dude* out and about. In fact, he told me he was upset because he expected me to "fix" his kids and I wasn't doing it!

One day, Jay's teen son was in the kitchen, and he said to Jay, "Either you get rid of her or I will." Jay's ex-wife had re-married, and his son had a relationship with his new stepfather. That day, Jay's son proceeded to call his stepfather who was part of a mafia mob; he requested his savings in order to hire a hit man to kill me. This stepfather is the one who molested Jay's daughter, and *in fact,* he had not only been charged with *incest,* but also for being involved in a child pornography film ring. Jay's kids had seen their mother held at gun-point by their stepfather; everyone in the family was scared to death of him, but she wouldn't leave him. Jay told me about his son's plan for me; he decided that it was best for us to separate and said, "Until the kids decide that they need you." Jay did have reason to warn me as he himself had been set up in the past by his children's stepfather (to be beat up). Jay had ended up with a ruptured bladder and was left for dead in an alley.

So, that was the beginning of a one-year separation; we were married a total of six years. I didn't file for the divorce, Jay did. It was out of convenience for himself. Jay had filed for food stamps and government assistance because he had lost his job. Government assistance was denied because he was still married to me, and I had several jobs. At the time I had my nursing position, I was doing consulting work and teaching college. I basically accepted any opportunities to substitute-teach and did the books at my sister's store (in order to support the kids and pay off debt). Jay got the divorce so he could receive government assistance. My sister helped me to find a new home to live in, but with all of the bills to pay, I don't know how I would have made it without our church helping us to make the move. We moved into an old country home (with rats crawling all about), but I felt more than ready for a fresh start! The church knew that Jay was still living in town and that he had asked me to leave. Their provision of food was so helpful!

My first husband, Joe, died of four different cancers related to HIV. After my second divorce and a couple of years past my first husband's death, I fell in love with another man—Luke. It was a mutually meaningful, Christian relationship. However, he was raised in a mid-American morally conservative family; we had to painfully part ways. Luke could not handle bringing into his family the dynamic of my son being homosexual. So, I remain very active and committed as a leader in my Christian Singles ministry.

Leaving my abusive relationships has brought me *profound peace, calmness, a stronger faith,* and *friends* that I would not have otherwise connected with. Living an abuse-free life has saved my life and my children's lives. It's a whole different world! Going through the abuse was horrific; yes, it was stupid on my part to get caught up in such messes. And I did cause a lot of pain to many loved ones, and for the longest time, I carried around that guilt. But now I know better *who* made the *wrong choices*—I have gained some wisdom.

I'm sad to say that I've noticed that the abuse affected my sons in a way that they have never been able to make a lifetime commitment in a relationship. Nevertheless, living without the abuse has shown me that I *am strong,* and it has allowed me to see God more as my Heavenly Father, not just as my Daddy (as when I was a child).

I have grown to a point that I have re-dedicated my life to Him. I've come to realize how BIG God really is and that He's not just my childhood salvation experience. I've learned that I'm all grown-up now and that I can maintain an adult spiritual relationship with Him. I am grateful for my prayer being answered—my *joy* has been *restored*, and so has my *gratitude* for God being in charge! I lived a very dangerous life, but I have reasons to continue living now.

If ever I meet anyone now that's involved in an abusive relationship, I say with *everything in me*, "Get out! Run! Get away! Get help—you can't walk through it alone. Find someone you trust and *run* for the safety of your life." I am currently as healthy as can be. I know now that God set me aside to save myself and to save other lives; He protected me from harm's way, including HIV.

My life nowadays is full of *hope* and *joy* because it just gurgles up in me all of the time. Even when memories get stirred up and I'm trying to have a pity party, He just doesn't let me! I can cry out and say, "God, all I wanted was to be a loving, Christian wife and for my children to have a Daddy, since I wasn't raised with one." Then I find myself thanking Him instead—that I am determined to live my life fully! I can't help but to want it that way.

There's *no room for bitterness* in my life now—just *joy*. I no longer question His timing for the events that took place in my past or present life. When I'm driving in my car and I think back on my painful past, it's immediately replaced by the joy within me in the present—and I even giggle to myself. I've learned that *I don't have to be accepted or approved* by *anyone* in this world—my life is between me and God.

PART III

HELPERS AND SOCIETY CAN OVERCOME ABUSE

Victim & Society Redemption
IT'S NOT JUST THE victims and *Overcomers* that are in need of healing; it's the entire body of politics in our society that are in need of repair! Exposing the abuser and victim not only takes care of our endangered society, but also acts as a means of catharsis for the *Overcomer*. She has successfully recovered from her victim role under the control of the abuser, but she has also gained the awareness and confidence that, in having resolutely confronted her abuser, she has overcome the most tragic of the consequences of abuse trauma. She broke her silence and spoke up and told him that he can no longer control her through fear and then stood up to expose him to the public and the legal system. Society needs to follow suit by learning to respond to

spousal and family abuse through a clear lens, acknowledging that it has to be faced and confronted.

Our culture needs to stop focusing on only acknowledging stranger assault. A victim's pain from spousal or family abuse is *no less real*. The fears are not less valid than being assaulted by a total stranger; it's actually *more* traumatizing for the victim to be betrayed by a trusted relationship. If victim abuse is to be defeated, society *must* make defense against any assailing danger—including spousal abuse. Society does have an influence statistically as to how many victims will choose to report family violence and work toward overcoming their abuse. Our nation has to support communities in recognizing that marital and family abuse *is* a community problem that *has* to have a community solution. In return, communities have to ascertain that society's need to end marital and family violence takes precedence, so that spousal and family abuse have no home in our society. Some states in the U.S. have communities that have developed family violence prevention programs and organizations, but this is not the case for all states.

And, even when communities have established family violence prevention programs, many citizens don't believe the victims, make excuses as to why they can't get involved, or worry about their own safety more so than about the victim's safety. This includes mandated reporters who have a motto of "stay out of it" or are simply uneducated about victim abuse and fail to meet their obligation to report it. "You have a nice day" has become the substitute for "shut up" when a person (even counselors) doesn't want to hear about the problem of abuse in our communities. Some states enthrone the idea that instead of the government getting involved in a marriage's "domestic violence" (a crime), the victim just has to find shelter (she has to leave her own home, sometimes her state), and maybe "the church"

HELPERS AND SOCIETY CAN OVERCOME ABUSE

can help out—but wait—then there's the issue of separation of church and state!

In some communities their laws give victims "nuisance" citations for placing a certain number of calls reporting the abuser and seeking help from the police. Some property owners use police assistance to evict victims who are a "nuisance" with domestic violence (DV) incidents and police calling. The majority of communities report that the police fail to take DV calls seriously. Most state police departments have units for homicide, drugs, robbery and other crimes; but they do not all have a police unit dedicated to DV. It is only in the larger cities that DV units are found (which is perfect for the abuser because he loves to isolate his victim away from police vigilance and DV charges). In the court system, even if a DV division exists, the victim is generally not offered supportive resources; for the focus is on the abuser being referred to counseling or other services.

Efforts and collaboration to enforce a *no tolerance* for family abuse is already set in *some* communities. Think of what our society would be like if our entire nation of communities responded in the same way. As fellow humans, our communities nationwide need to join forces with local and state governments, law enforcement, district attorneys, probation officers, legal and business leaders, boards of education, faith leaders, mental and medical health professionals, lay volunteers, and family violence advocacy organizations to judicially address spousal and family abuse. Our nation—not just the abuser—needs to begin to view women from the lens of *respect*. Healing is not just necessary for the victim. Our culture needs to lead the way for women to not be exploited through technology, in the community, and in the workplace. The media itself provides an opportunity for women to be constantly eye-raped; our culture can heal from this perversion only with the cooperation and redemption of society's view of women.

Legal responsibility to victims in our society is of utmost relevance. Public awareness has to be set in place along with educational opportunities about family abuse. Records and statistics need to be updated and maintained in a database that can keep the communities and our society informed on the progress being made to resolve the problem of family abuse. The database is useful in assessing the needs for education, healthcare, law enforcement, and legal aid to victims of abuse. Communities must develop family violence prevention programs, organizations, and campaigns against family abuse. Collecting a database can be done with the same approach used in the 1960's when an advisory committee to the U.S. Surgeon General got together to gather records and statistics on smoking and health. The report had a permanent change within the U.S. and the world with a response that changed attitudes and behaviors toward cigarette smoking. The report of the correlation between cigarette smoking and lung cancer and other respiratory illnesses led to perspective and policy changes on the act of cigarette smoking. Further, the development of warning labels, anti-smoking campaigns, and restrictions on tobacco advertising went into effect.

In 2014, the U.S. Surgeon General released a call to action regarding the major cause of skin cancer (overexposure to indoor/outdoor ultraviolent light). FDA labels in tanning salons are now to be visible, and public awareness notices and steps to protect skin are to be posted. Even urban planners are being instructed to provide shaded areas for the public. Cigarette smoking and skin cancer warnings are about health and saving lives. The problem of family violence is also about health and death. It is becoming more difficult to gather updated research data on abuse of women and children because in contemporary society administrative forms are being designed as gender neutral; which interferes with the reliability of the conclusion in abuse reports. Is there any reason the U.S. Surgeon General and an advisory committee can't gather together the reliable database to raise public awareness, campaigns, restrictions, and instructions with policy changes on family violence?

There are so many possibilities for public awareness and prevention of abuse campaigns that could be initiated, put into place, and acted upon. These campaigns can include obtainable goals and strategies with an outcome as follows but would not be limited to: teaching communities not to marginalize women and children and not to normalize abuse which only serves to create an abuse enabling society; offer employer mandatory workshops on abuse; create educational community mobilization activities; improve and strengthen resource referral mechanisms; create family violence specialized services through trained service providers; enhance abuser and victim abuse knowledge within the police and court system; create updated true story films to educate families and the public on abuse; improve research on our modern society's attitudes toward abuse and victims of abuse; update causes of abuse, it's sustained prevalence, and its consequences on the victims and society; release research data with the most current surveys' conclusive evidence of violence and a violation against women and children's human rights reports and its implications on the victims and our nation; and engage legal and policy makers in confronting abuse on all levels and addressing the current research with the intent to reform laws to allow victims' justice and abusers the lawful consequences for their emotional and or physical crimes.

There's a lot of ballyhoo advertising for advanced technology, cars, food, alcohol, and toys, all of which are worthless without the sanctity of human life. The most prominent ads are saved for during the Olympics, the Super Bowl, and Hollywood awards. Why can't the real-life problem of family abuse be advocated for with help information provided during primetime TV programs? Is it because the real dark side of family abuse, which takes place daily, cannot interrupt for sixty seconds the unrealistic TV excitement that's not a part of everyday family living? Are the half-time shows that display soft porn dancing and the devaluation of women as men's entitled entertainment and the distorted and disturbing role modeling to boys and girls of women's role; what America will continue to use as prime-time TV? Are the money-maker gatekeepers responsible for only allowing unrealistic, happy-all-the-time family life ads during primetime? Yes, there's progress on TV commercials about drug use and suicide prevention and teen pregnancy assistance; however, there's silence on preventing family violence. There are even very graphic ads depicting facial and throat deformities resulting from smoking and chewing tobacco cancer; however, there's silence on the swollen, bruised faces and mangled bodies of shaken victims.

How about some primetime commercials on preventing family violence with vigorous referrals to victim hotlines? An initiative—with follow through—has to take place to inundate viewers with messages through YouTube and social media—with an outcry on *how* to stop victim and family abuse. Healthy, functional family living can be promoted and advertised! What about using primetime to put aside some of the provocative TV commercials that depict sexual innuendoes and instead to air some family violence prevention commercials? If our society is going to become aware and knowledgeable about the gravity and pandemic nature of abuse trauma in our nation, the internet, social media, movie theaters, and TV must be saturated with education on the abuser and victim dynamics. We live in an abuse-sustained planet because of denial and ignorance to the dynamics of abuse. Electronic and hard copy literature has to be made available to use as resources to educate communities, victims, and abusers on the dynamics and ramifications of abuse trauma.

There are billboard ads for adult shops that sell racy lingerie and sex toys, X-rated (porn) video stores, and gentlemen's

HELPERS AND SOCIETY CAN OVERCOME ABUSE

clubs—why not billboard ads offering resource contacts against family violence? If our society is going to be educated on and stop abuse trauma in our nation, the resource brochures have to be made available and placed in prominent public facilities to be used as literature, which will educate communities and victims on the dynamics and consequences of abuse and in addition provide contact resource information for victims to obtain assistance. Professional development courses and seminars must be well-advertised notifying educators, first responders, mental health professionals, and faith leaders.

Studies reveal that victims are at their greatest risk of assault when they report their abuse to police, after they threaten to leave, or leave their abusive domicile. Research in the U.S. has shown that victims who leave their abuser are at a seventy-five percent greater risk of being killed by their abusers than those who stay. In 2003 J.C. Campbell, D. Webster, J. Koziol-McLain, and others conducted a controlled study which concluded that the presence of a weapon in the home of an abusive relationship increases the risk of homicide by five hundred percent. The Federal Bureau of Investigation US Department of Justice *Uniform Crime Reporting Program Data: Supplementary Homicide Reports* revealed that in 2013, fifty percent of the approximately 1,270 intimate partner homicides in the United States were committed with firearms.

The organization *Everytown for Gun Safety* gathered data from media reports and official public records and developed a mass shooting report which analyzed 173 mass shootings in the United States from 2009-2017. The *Everytown* study found and concluded in their report that one of the factors which contribute to mass shootings *is* domestic/family violence. Their analysis revealed the shootings included eighty-six percent of mass shooting child fatalities.

In the 2013 U.S. Department of Justice, Bureau of Justice Statistics Report, it was estimated that 503,485 U.S. victims are stalked by their abuser each year. An organization and program, similar to the Amber or elderly (Silver) Alerts, could be established by communities: whenever a person suspected to be a victim of abuse is reported as being stalked or missing—instead of waiting to hear of her murder on the news—send out a Purple Alert! A firm, active, and genuine commitment from communities to eliminate family violence provides a comprehensive outreach to victims that are striving to *overcome* abuse for their sake, their future family generations, and our society.

Furthermore, it is our spiritual duty to our next of kin or community to remind or notify the victim that Jesus is alive and ready to deliver her from her abuse. The victim needs to hear from you that Jesus, in Person, walked the Earth to deliver the victim *and* her children out of her captivity. He didn't just walk around to shake hands like a politician; He actually came in order to fulfill His promises! He said: "The Spirit of the Lord is upon Me, because He has anointed Me to preach the gospel to the poor. He has sent Me to heal the brokenhearted, to preach deliverance to the captives and recovery of sight to the blind, to set at liberty those who are oppressed" (Luke 4:18). Victims may continue to suffer *enduringly* because they have either ignored or are confused about the nature and extent of Jesus' mission here on Earth. It is your role as the victim's advocate to share or review Jesus' mission for her life.

In addition to Jesus's mission of revealing His identity to us as our Lord and Savior, He came to tell us about His mission of love and redemption. As the Anointed One, He preached the gospel to the poor. The word poor refers to those who are either poor due to low economic status and/or those who are in bondage by spiritual poverty (Matthew 5:3, Luke 6:20). Apart from God's *spiritual intervention,* we can do nothing eternal. What does not

HELPERS AND SOCIETY CAN OVERCOME ABUSE

originate from God's love and Kingdom doesn't last on Earth. Our own intellect, skills, and talents aren't lasting or powerful enough to divinely *overcome* (Zechariah 4:6). Remind the victim that God does promise her His everlasting love and redemption for the rest of her days!

There are victims who remain in their abusive relationships because they are in bondage, feeling unable to financially provide for themselves and their family if they leave their abuser. All victims that feel economically entrapped (whether they come from a lower-, middle-, or upper-class) experience their abuser as tarnishing any fleeting hope of happiness or peace in their daily thoughts about the life they live. Plans and dreams are on standby or thwarted as the relationship rots and deteriorates. It becomes apparent to the victim that dreams are just dreams with an abuser because none of the dreams that he or she have voiced will ever come true, as she realizes that the abuser will never act on them. While in bondage, the victim tries to fix the relationship in a world that says, "Do not address wife abuse" (even knowing that there is a large part of the world that lives happily in non-abusive marriages). Or, she may join the ranks of numberless victims that must, for the sake of safety and sanity, leave their home without any resources and may end up on the streets homeless.

It is only the restoration of *hope* and *peace* that unshackles the victim and allows her to believe that she can be free of her abuser's economic controlling grip and indeed overcome her abuse. She now realizes that her abuser's monetary power and evil, oppositional behavior toward her does not have to be tolerated and that she does not have to live surrounded by an abusive marriage—that she can triumph as an *Overcomer*. You can help to instill that hope to overcome within her. Once she has faith, she has hope, which keeps her abuse in perspective and which vanquishes all of her fears so she can proceed to experience living a peace-empowered, victorious life. Experiencing faith instills hope in the *Overcomer* who now believes in the invisible and recognizes that hope accomplishes the impossible—even while undergoing economic deprivation because she knows nothing is impossible for Him! Hope infuses peace into her spirit. Having faced her painful marital abuse, she wins over her abuser's economic control over her. She has availed herself of the opportunity to choose a life of peace over being disempowered into victimization. According to the Department of Justice, family violence infests the lives of millions of Americans—a crime that affects people from all walks of life. Won't you help a victim of abuse restore her hope and peace in her life?

What can a Lay Person do When Abuse is Suspected?
Most victims do not have a clue where to turn to when they've realized that they're being abused. Or, in other cases, they've reached their limit on their abuse, but they may have had a bad experience when they sought assistance from someone. As a helper, you have vast resources in literature, on the internet, and in God for all of the work He wants you to accomplish with victims of abuse. Your willingness to act as a helper on her behalf can be a matter of life and death for that victim and/or her children. Your positive response when she reaches out to you for help can directly influence her efforts to engage in a safety plan. However, your willingness to help, although kind and generous and your motive pure, is not sufficient to provide help. Preparing yourself to provide the kind of help that she needs is the best help she can get!

The short- and long-term effects of victim abuse have far-reaching spiritual, emotional, and physical consequences. The symptoms of victim abuse vary from victim to victim. Nevertheless, learning some of the symptoms and possible indicators of victim abuse and their effects on the victim will assist

HELPERS AND SOCIETY CAN OVERCOME ABUSE

you in comprehending her experience, as well as help you to more quickly identify a victim of abuse. Victims are genius about covering up any type of abuse except for their physical abuse because it becomes evident in their body. Below are some physical signs:

- Consistently despondent facial affect.
- Multiple bruises/injuries in various healing stages.
- Excuses or unexplained delay in seeking treatment for injuries.
- Bruises, burns, lacerations, swollen areas, human teeth marks, and fractures—especially in the facial areas.
- Premature births during pregnancy, miscarriages/abortions.
- Anxiety, depression, stress or addiction-related illnesses, including eating disorders.

The symptoms are listed as signs because most victims will not use the word or confess "abuse." The victim's common approach (if at all) is to disclose a *presenting problem* (which is truly related to the abuse), either coming from or affecting her household or place of employment such as:

- Marital or family discord.
- Drug and or other addictions.
- Mental health challenges.
- Harassment by her abuser at work over the internet, on the phone, or in person.
- History of job-hopping/loss of employment.
- Lack of incentive to work, low production, frequent requests to take time off work, being late or a no-show at work.

The best way to identify if someone is being abused is to ask. A victim will talk about her abuse if you reassure her of confidentiality; the only reason victims hide their abuse is because of fear of their abusers finding out they told. They are embarrassed and also fear the person they tell will not believe them, may blame them for staying, or may suggest that they get out of the abuse when they are unable to follow through. Asking a suspected victim in private without imposing judgment if she's being abused relieves her of the loathsome burden of her being the one to initiate disclosure. This approach requires the person to approach her without the expectation that she will immediately disclose with trust. If you approach her without any expectations of full disclosure, she will feel that the reason for your question is because you care, are genuinely concerned, and are willing to help.

Sometimes you won't have to ask the victim if she is being abused; you may suspect or learn that she has left her spouse. Do not judge her or give her advice. A spouse that has to escape does not leave because of a tiff or even several tiffs. Generally, an escapee leaves because she has endured any of or all of the types of abuse, does not feel emotionally and/or physically safe, and no longer wants to live that way.

Keep your question simple. Interject that you have noticed a symptom(s) and share that you are concerned and want to offer if there's something that you can do to help. Reassure her that if she wants to talk now or set up a day to talk that you will keep her conversation confidential. Our society raises people to believe that they need not get involved in other people's business and that what happens in other people's homes or lives is something to stay out of. Therefore, most people think that a suspected victim will not welcome their concern and see it as prying. However, the notion to "stay out of" someone else's business has only contributed to the increased isolation of victims of abuse and has resulted in the inability of victims to feel free to seek help and support. You taking a risk by asking about her abuse—and the possibility of her rejecting your question—is minor compared to the risk of her isolation with her abuser.

HELPERS AND SOCIETY CAN OVERCOME ABUSE

Naturally, it is imperative that if you do take that opportunity to ask if she's being abused that you are sincere and prepared to respond in a supportive and actively helpful way. The list of what you can do to learn to prepare yourself to assist a victim of abuse is endless, but whatever you can do is sure to empower her by way of your assistance! Here are some possible interventions:

First above all, take a crash course and educate yourself on domestic violence—with time, you can always come back and learn more. There are numerous resources on the internet, or you can make an appointment to get the basics from a victim advocate. Learn what resources and services are available for the victim.

- Confront yourself on any abuse triggers, biases, stereotypes, or erroneous beliefs you may have about victims of abuse.
- Substitute any negative thoughts that stopping the abuse is hopeless with positive thoughts about the courage, mindfulness, industriousness, resourcefulness, decision-making potential, and resilience of victims of abuse, which can be used as a strength in being better able to help the victim.
- Validate the fact that she doesn't choose abuse, that there's nothing wrong with her, and that she is not to blame but rather that she has become ensnared and has been in captivity by a controlling, coercive abuser.
- Relinquish any expectations or desires that you will be able to fix the obstacles or abuse the victim is experiencing. Give her flexibility and understanding for inaction because it's a matter of the best strategy for her safety, day-by-day.

The most important intervention that you will use to open up the doorway for her to accept help is to let her know that you believe her. Tell her that you understand that abusers act appropriately in public, but not in the privacy of their home. Listen to her intently so that you can learn directly from her what kind of help she needs, but do ask questions for clarity. Learn if there are any weaknesses and only build on her strengths; use the positive coping and problem-solving skills she has even if her efforts have failed in the past. Encourage her to try again and build on those skills.

It's impossible to help a victim of abuse if you do not validate her feelings. Sometimes you will be validating thoughts and feelings that are in sync with what she's experiencing, and other times you will be validating feelings of confusion between love and fear; hopelessness and fantasies of reconciliation; and guilt, anger, and unforgiveness. Validate these feelings of grief and despair. Accept her fears as legitimate and help her to take her fears seriously by saying that you believe she's in danger and that you are concerned for her safety. Do not victim-blame her. Reiterate that the abuse is her boyfriend's or spouse's choice and that he has to take responsibility for his behaviors—not her. However, do not speak condemningly about him.

Offer to become active in formulating her safety plan. Suggest to her that you will stand by her as she takes on her problem of abuse, considers all of her safe options, and evaluates the risks and benefits (pros and cons). Tell her that you will help her to identify ways that she can reduce the safety risks. Offer ideas, information you have learned about abuse, and resources. Offer to help, but only do what you feel comfortable in assisting with. If there are things you are unable to help with, ask her in what other ways you can assist her into safety. Whatever decisions she chooses to make regarding her abuse, accept those decisions because every decision a victim of abuse makes is centered on protecting herself and calculated around safety. The best way any person can help a victim of abuse is to respect her person, even if you question her decisions. But do not be shy about sharing with her the good news about overcoming her abuse and the hope, joy, and peace she deserves to experience as an *Overcomer*!

Sometimes, the only way you will be able to help her when she refuses assistance is to pray to God that He would hasten the day that she will gain wise insight about her abuse. Praying for a victim of abuse, her safety and protection, is like working for Christ in Secret Service. Pray for others that might interact with the victim that God's Spirit would work with His unusual supernatural power in them to minister to her about overcoming her abuse. Enlist Christ as her protective vanguard. Through your ongoing prayers, you can become an army of protective assistance for the victim.

Overall, it's simple to do something for a suspected victim of abuse: ask, listen, and validate, express concern, offer to assist, support whatever decisions she makes about her abuse, and pray for her. Remember not to wait for her to initiate self-disclosure, but don't pressure her into disclosure, either. Never judge, condemn, or blame; provide only supportive, unconditional assistance. In this way, lay persons are the unsung heroes and heroines who open the victim's heart to consider overcoming her abuse—leading her to the path of freedom from abuse. It is because of these unsung acts of service that a victim's story changes and she becomes a part of God's life story. Lay persons that help victims of abuse become God's fellow workers.

When abuse is suspected, should this work of doing something about the suspected abuse be left up to women advocates? No. Are there men in the community that are willing to take the risk of confronting victims and men about their abuse? Yes. There are men that are willing to listen and to take seriously the reality that a victim of abuse lives. When women deny men the opportunity to be accountable with respect for women and children (or the ability to gently ask the victim about her abuse or to confront the abuser), then these working men in the community will not be willing to intervene or to make the necessary changes as advocates to stop the abuse or to validate a victim of abuse. In turn, why would male abusers come forward and become responsible in respecting women and children?

Domestic Violence in the Military—How Can You Help?
You may live in a military community; your neighbor(s) or you yourself may even be in the military or have military family. How can you help if you suspect victim abuse? The dynamics, symptoms, and consequences of abuse trauma are no different for military victims. All the helper has to do is educate him/herself on how domestic violence is dealt with and treated in the military and then offer to help. The following is some information on how spousal abuse is intervened upon in the military:

Under the Uniform Code of Military Justice (UCMJ), domestic violence is a crime, which can be prosecuted by court martial. Historically, military officials prosecuted spousal abuse under the general justice categories, such as assault. The penalty included prison time and a dishonorable discharge from the military. However, domestic violence in the military was researched, and analysts concluded that the general justice categories did not match the seriousness of the abusive offenses.

This decision to treat domestic violence as a specific, separate crime under military law included the assistance of civilian law enforcement agents who suggested military officials establish greater domestic violence military policy and procedure measures. Civilian advocates contributed the fact that since domestic violence did not have a specific crime penalty under military law, civilian law enforcement was unable to track the military once they were discharged.

It was noted that because the military was not convicting domestic violence as a separate crime from other assaults, the military records which the civilian authorities had access to did not reveal the at-risk military discharged abuser who could be a future firearms carrier or purchaser once out of the military. The military is now able to report to outside law enforcement when a service member has had a record of domestic violence, and therefore civilian authorities are able to have a list of prior service members' domestic crimes and disqualify them from purchasing firearms. The military also has a system in place to defend, protect, and safely transfer the domestic violence or sexual assault victim away from her abuser and to offer her resources. In 2017, a Blue Star Family survey found that fifteen percent of military family members did not feel physically safe in their current relationship.

It's important to note that in the military, "domestic abuse" and "domestic violence" are defined differently.

Domestic abuse is a broader term which includes any and all types of harmful emotional/physical violence against a victim from a former or current intimate relationship or a spouse. Domestic abuse in the military is defined as a pattern of behavior resulting in emotional/psychological abuse and/or an interference with personal liberty. Some of the terms used for domestic abuse include "spousal neglect," "economic abuse," "sexual abuse," and "harassment."

Domestic violence is a term used by the military under the UCMJ to identify a crime which involves the threatened, attempted, or use of force or violence against a victim from a former intimate relationship or a current spouse. It is considered domestic violence if a lawful order, such as a military protective order (MPO) or civil protection order (CPO) is violated. Both the MPO and CPO require that the abuser stay away from the victim, her children, her workplace/school, her home/other places of activity, and to refrain from committing any acts of abuse/violence against the victim.

The Family Advocacy Program (FAP) is a Department of Defense (DOD) organization that assists families through military and civilian agencies with mental health care, including domestic violence and child abuse. The goals of FAP include, but are not limited to: providing education on abuse, prevention of family abuse, identification of unhealthy relationship patterns/abuse and prompt reporting, providing treatment for victims and their families, and to advocate and promote victim empowerment and safety. Upon request, the victim and children can receive clinical treatment, support, resource referrals, and safety planning services. Even a civilian victim who is being abused by a military service member can receive FAP care.

Victims of military abusers can report domestic abuse/violence to their own command or the abuser's commander, military law enforcement, FAP, or any healthcare provider. However, it's pertinent to understand that where the victim first reports the abuse will determine if the incident will be documented as "unrestricted" (meaning an investigation will follow) or if it is reported as "restricted" (meaning an official investigation does not follow).

If an abuse incident is first reported to military/civilian law enforcement and/or command, it becomes an unrestricted report, which means the criminal investigation includes a referral for an assessment and safety planning by FAP. If the abuse incident is first reported to FAP, the victim can elect a restricted report and no civilian or military authorities/command will be notified of the incident (no investigation will take place). The exception is if there's a high risk of harm to the victim or others. Both unrestricted and restricted reporting provide the victim with access to military benefits such as medical care and FAP services.

The difference between the domestic violence response of the military and civilian agencies is the authority the commanding officer has over the abuser. The commanding officer has the authority to use administrative, judicial, or other penalties to respond to the reported abuse. Most commanders contact a Staff Judge Advocate (military attorney) to consult and evaluate what the charge is under the UCMJ and what the discipline will be. Possible actions against the abuser that can take place after he is reported to his commander include as follows: an administrative decision that no action is warranted, a full military inspection and investigation, forfeiture of pay, a demotion, criminal charges, imprisonment and discharge from the service.

If the abuser is a civilian and the victim is military, the commander is limited in confronting the abuser through the UCMJ. The commander can restrict the abuser from entering the installation and, as most installations have military law enforcement at the entrance and exit, the MPs (military police) at the gate would be notified of the restriction. However, it's also recommended that a military victim with a civilian abuser secure civilian legal services along with a CPO and safety planning with FAP. A victim can have both an MPO and CPO in place at the same time. However, a victim must be aware that if she lives in the community, civilian law enforcement cannot legally enforce an MPO; all the civilian authority can do is contact the abuser's command to notify them that the MPO was violated. That's why it is important for a victim who does not reside in a military installation to also have a CPO—because civilian authorities can enforce them.

The main difference between an MPO and a CPO is the procedure in obtaining the order and the length of time that the order will be in place. Some victims opt for both an MPO and CPO but seek assistance in civilian agencies/shelters where the confidentiality codes of ethics are legally stricter and apply according to federal, state, and local laws and domestic violence policies. Most civilian agencies and shelters are trained in military and civilian domestic violence practices. No notice is required for an MPO to be served, and it does not give the abuser a right to a hearing or the right to testify; there's no "due process" when an MPO is issued. An MPO is therefore short-term in comparison to a CPO, but if the victim works with an advocate, a commander can structure the MPO to the specific time frame for the "no contact" safety needs of the victim and her children.

In the military, there are only three groups of professionals who have the authority to maintain confidentiality about domestic abuse under the "restricted" policy. These are the victim advocates, FAP clinicians, and medical professionals. Nevertheless, these professionals must report the abuse to military law enforcement and command if they determine that reporting is necessitated for the purpose of reducing or preventing an immediate threat to the health and safety of the victim and others. The military also grants confidential communication with a chaplain.

How to Help a Victim of Digital Abuse
Technology-facilitated abuse/digital abuse is the use of devices to either—unbeknownst to the victim—follow her or directly communicate to intimidate, harass, bully, or simply control the victim via texts, emails, apps, or GPS. The abuser may use the apps and malware to keep track of the victim's location, activities, and communication with anyone outside of himself.

Misuse of technology in unhealthy premarital and marital relationships is a growing type of abuse. Numerous civilian and military domestic violence organizations are reporting the provision of technology-specific advocacy and services for victims of abuse. Habitual misuse of technology in a relationship is domestic abuse. There is cause for concern when a victim has already informed the abuser that she does not want to be followed or to share her location with him, yet he deceives her and persists by secretly following her activity. When this limit has been

HELPERS AND SOCIETY CAN OVERCOME ABUSE

communicated yet trespassed by the abuser, it's time for the victim to begin documenting his digital abuse and to do something about it.

If you observe or she confides that her abuser has been misusing technology to keep track of her or harassing or intimidating her via his electronic device, inform and validate to her that it *is* digital abuse. Assist her in learning how to log her abuser's behavior, for the purpose of developing a technology safety plan. A sample of a Technology Abuse Log created by the National Network to End Domestic Violence, Safety Net Project, is provided in the Resources section of this book. By logging her abuser's misuse of technology, she can document his patterns of digital abuse which will be useful information for her and her helper or advocate in developing a technology safety plan. Why develop a technology safety plan? The purpose of a technology safety plan is to reduce any further or future harm. In the military, a technology log serves as evidence if the victim elects to file an unrestricted report of abuse. Instruct the victim to save everything that pertains to the abusive behaviors; but not to save all of her data in the same format or location. And certainly not in the same electronic device she shares with her abuser. Have her include records of phone calls, voice messages, unexpected sharing location notices on her phone, texts, emails, social media posts, and physical notes.

The following are important digital abuse points of record for the victim to document:

- **Maintain a written log.** Document the day, date, time, location, type of electronic device used, and a brief description of the incident. Note any witnesses. Save this record in any format that will not become accessible to the abuser.
- **Save emails from original accounts.** The abuser may delete emails or delete his name after forwarding his original

email; so screenshot or print emails with header information immediately upon discovery. It's important to include the header because it identifies the sender.
- **Download/Screenshot/Photograph Social Media Info.** Screenshot the abuser's profile page. Document details of stalking or specific abusive posts right away, including the full URL in the window bar at the top, lest the abuser deletes. If your social media account allows or via the use of an app, download the data you have screenshot.
- **Screenshot or Photograph Text Messages.** Include the phone contact page which shows the phone number connected to the name on the text message.
- **Screenshot and/or print telephone call logs.** Document voice mails. State laws vary on recording telephone conversations; if allowed to record, do so.
- **Document all that is evidence of digital abuse.** Take strong safety precautions on the physical location for storing evidence. If it's not safe or secure to store in the victim's electronic devices or household; it's best to ask a trusted person to privately file the data.

If the victim is going to file criminal charges, assist her in preparing her technology abuse evidence for the court hearing. Once she has filed charges, an attorney or law enforcement can request or subpoena a website or social media company to save your and your abuser's account information as evidence. Caution the victim and instill in her that safety is the priority. Abusers usually escalate when their digital abuse or any deceitful abusive acts are discovered. If she discovers that she is being digitally monitored/stalked via a hidden microphone/camera or GPS tracker, she must refrain from disconnecting or removing such equipment. The impact on the victim when the abuser finds out she has discovered his tracking equipment could endanger her. Also, removing the abuser's tracking devices restricts her from logging the incidents and documenting her evidence. A safer approach to removing monitoring/stalking equipment is to contact law enforcement and have them document the evidence, followed up by an appointment with an abuse advocate, to strategize a safety plan, and the removal of the abuser's tracking equipment.

Prior to gathering her evidence for court, remind the victim that there are technologies that have been set up to automatically delete digital information after it has been viewed; this makes it increasingly difficult to retrieve the abuser's information as evidence. Therefore, the victim must have a strategic plan on how she will access the information. Make sure that she is aware that *some apps may alert the sender* (abuser) of her screenshot or recording his information; be sure she researches well her safety risks in gathering her digital evidence. Furthermore, instruct her that there's a protocol on how the digital evidence is presented in court. For instance, the judge will not allow her to just bring her own electronic devices with all of her gathered evidence in it. Allowing her to present her case through her own device puts her at risk for her device to be taken as evidence; she has to gather her data in a form that the court allows.

That being said, she must save all screenshots onto her phone, tablet, or desktop as a photo image with the purpose of printing them out for the court hearing. While printing any images for the court as well as emails, she must ascertain that the headers show relevant data on the sender, dates, time, and all identifying information. If the court hearing is set far in advance and the victim feels highly at risk for safety, she may want to notify law enforcement of her threatening messages or emails so that they are able to investigate the abuser before the court hearing. If it is an abusive tweet, she does have the right to report the abusive message and to request an email report of the threatening tweet; this report will provide her with the date and time of the tweet, her account data, the username of the person who tweeted, and the date and time of her report.

As a backup, she may want to email or text message herself photo images of all her printed documents to her secure device. She can also record a video of her text messages if there are a large number of them. Videotaping abusive messages is useful on apps whose messages quickly disappear and which also notify the sender if she does screenshot. Obviously, she will be able to print her screenshots, but she will need a video player to present her recorded evidence. Encourage her to talk to her abuse advocate or attorney about the laws in her state regarding accepting videos as evidence in court and the type of video file the court is able to play. It's a crime in some states to record a phone conversation. If recorded evidence of a voicemail is allowed in her state, she can save it onto a CD or DVD to present to the court. Some states do not allow recorded evidence without the permission of everyone (including the abuser) participating in the recording. The court always requires advance notice if video or voice recording will be presented as evidence. Audio recordings, if allowed in her state, can be accessed and recorded through her phone or a classic mini tape recorder.

And while on the subject of recording voicemails or documenting conversations, be certain that she is thorough in retrieving complete conversations (consecutive multiple messages/incidents) because the court will make a decision based on the entire story and not just on partial messages. In addition to recorded conversations or logged in incidents, she must provide a full profile on the abuser, which she can easily retrieve from his social media, business/career profile. The court looks for the complete story as to what the abuser has done and what has happened to the victim; a compilation of a single voicemail, text, or email may not be sufficient evidence to prove a persistent,

HELPERS AND SOCIETY CAN OVERCOME ABUSE

controlling pattern of digital harassment, threatening, or stalking behaviors.

Now that she has gathered all of her digital abuse evidence, review with her once again how crucial it is that she saves and stores all of her data in a place that the abuser has no access to. Even if she's confident that he does not have her login/password and thinks he cannot capture her evidence, she may still want to move her evidence to a safer file. The last step after she has retrieved all of the harassing messages or incidents by taking screenshots, photographs, printing the evidence, or placing the voice recording, or videotaping in the formats that the court will accept as evidence, is to double check her state's laws (because they change quickly). This research of her state's laws is in her best interest in order for the court's "rules of evidence" to assist the judge and jury in providing her with justice. Recommend to her that she read the step-by-step guide on how to present evidence in a court of law, *10 Steps for Presenting Evidence in Court* https://www.rcdvcpc.org/resources/ resource/10-steps-for-presenting-evidencein-court.html.

Informing yourself as a helper on what to look for in an abuser's technology-facilitated control of the victim is one way to understand and assist the victim. Encourage the victim, reassuring her that it's not her fault that her abuser is using an unsafe approach to technology. Overprotecting and over-caring about a person with whom there's a romantic or spousal relationship can become "controlling" behavior, and it makes the victim feel unsafe in the relationship. A victim who is involved in a relationship with a person who has an excessive habit of checking phone logs, texting, emailing, following on social media, or tracking the victim's activity has a serious, unhealthy relationship pattern—a disrespectful abuse habit. The abuser is a tech safety-risk in the relationship and is misusing technology to control the relationship and the victim's identity.

Some examples of unhealthy tracking behaviors which indicate the abuser is misusing technology to disrespect and control the victim are:

- Privacy Violations—In any kind of relationship, each person has a right to privacy. The decision to share phone calls, texts, emails, personal IDs, passwords, and social media accounts should always be mutual. A person who secretly follows, expects/demands a history of activity, reads personal messages, and/or checks phone logs is humiliating and exploiting the victim; he may attempt to intimidate with the information and is exhibiting insecure possessive and controlling behaviors.
- Emotional Abuse—It is emotional abuse when the person lies about her to others or talks about her in negative or offensive ways via texts, emails, or messaging apps/social media. It is abusive when she receives negative, derogatory, intimidating messages or passive-aggressive threats from him, sometimes even knowing she's in the middle of her scheduled activities. She dreads being followed (stalked) and fears receiving electronic messages from him.
- Unrequested Sharing of Location—If the person she is in an intimate relationship with or her spouse is tracking her location when she does not want to be tracked, this is controlling behavior and considered stalking. Stalking is a crime.
- Unrequested Sharing of Personal Data—The person she's in a relationship with shares her images/videos, texts, or emails without her consent.
- Forcing Explicit Content—The person manipulates, pressures, and forces her to share sexually explicit images/content; this is a form of sexual coercion.

HELPERS AND SOCIETY CAN OVERCOME ABUSE

How does a helper determine if the abuser is misusing technology to control the victim? It's as simple as asking the victim how she feels about her boyfriend's or spouse's use of technology that involves her. If she answers that she feels he is using technology to control her, then there's an unhealthy, abusive relationship. The best way to assist her in examining her unhealthy relationship is to explore with her what a healthy relationship looks like when technology is used.

In a healthy relationship, a person has a right to feel respected and safe both in person or online. Both people should be able to feel positively empowered and not disempowered by technology. The mutual agreement is that there is open communication and no defensive or angry tone is used when the other expresses a clear boundary and an expectation about limits on technology use within the relationship. No one should ignore or forbid conversations about which technology behaviors cross the line. In a healthy relationship, she should be able to feel free to:

- Maintain her personal ID/login and passwords' privacy.
- Say no to requests for location or sending or sharing any digital information.
- Say no to sending or receiving digital contents that make her feel uncomfortable.
- Set her privacy settings on activities or devices and to choose if she wants to accept any tags in photo sharing on social media.
- Decide if, how, or when anything about her is posted or communicated via text/email/social media.

Victim Abuse can be Overcome one Victim at a Time

Victims who become *Overcomers* are inspirited to encourage other victims to rise to the occasion of putting a stop to their abuse. However, they are not the only ones who can encourage a victim and produce change. There's more than one approach and solution to victim community outreach. Lay persons or neighbors who choose *not* to get *involved* in the phenomenon of victim abuse can also become instruments of change. This stance is similar to folks who say they don't feel called or don't have the flexibility to do missions work but they do have the means to donate to missions and do so.

Lay persons can do the same by donating a copy of *Volume I and/or II Overcoming Abuse: Embracing Peace Your Encyclopedic Guide to Freedom from Abuse* to their public or church library. Or, lay persons can donate a copy of *Volume I and/or II* to their local domestic violence organization. Ask for *Volume I* and/or *II* to be put in the hands of a victim because, more than likely, that victim will return to her abuser (the consequences of a victim returning to her abuser can be disastrous). However, if by chance *Volume I and II* is placed in the hands of a victim that is near ready to leave her abuser, you will have started her on the path to stop her abuse.

If you're wondering if it's God's will for you to help a victim because you don't feel qualified, it is. A lot of the people called by God in the Bible to serve a purpose did not feel qualified, but God equipped them for what He called them to do. He can do the same for you.

If donating a copy of *Volume I* or *II* to your local library or domestic violence organization is not for you, there's another way you can help victims of abuse. You can turn your concerned desire to help and uncertainty into energetic, written action! How about writing a letter about the problem of victim abuse (and the lax laws) to your federal lawmakers this week? Don't put it off until someday. For a victim of abuse, someday may be too late. Choose whether you want to write to a lawmaker in the Senate or House of Representatives. The post office has the correct names and addresses of your U.S. Senators and a listing of the Districts and Representatives. This is not to say that any

HELPERS AND SOCIETY CAN OVERCOME ABUSE

of these victim helper approaches are suitable for you in advocating for victims of abuse. God will lead you to the advocacy intervention that's right for you.

Even committing to pray for women and children who are entrapped as victims of abuse is a way to help victims of abuse. Many people are not willing or don't feel called to use their feet to assist victims, but they can reach out to them through their mouths in prayer. Tremendous work with victims can be accomplished by prayer. Prayers, whether voiced for victims in the U.S. or overseas or both, can achieve eternal work in penetrating satan's abusive lines of defense. In the area of abuse, satan's dark strongholds have scarcely been challenged by individuals who stand back and allow abuse to permeate our society from one generation to the next.

For centuries, satan has been allowed to blind the public about abuse and to prevent deliverance and healing from abuse. Because the public has been blind sighted about the dynamics of abuse, victims continue to flounder in confusion, as if abuse is a normal part of daily living ... just one of life's relationship problems. It's time for all people to take the place of the fallen defender, the victim, as supportive advocates! Won't you stand in the gap and disallow abuse of any type to transfuse into our current and future generations?

As long as some form of work is done to help a victim of abuse, you are doing good servant's work for God's Kingdom. The fruit of kindness is all that is needed to help out a victim of abuse—you don't have to say much—kindness is an unspoken gesture. The Bible tells the story of the beat-up, wounded traveler whom others passed by, but the good Samaritan had compassion on him and stopped to help out (Luke 10:30-33). Realize that as an advocate for victims of abuse, if you take the first step to help a victim of abuse, you are in essence surrendering your service into God's Hands. He will supply and multiply the work that you do for a victim; He will use your work as His work in and through the victim.

My prayer is that through the *Overcoming Abuse* book series, the Lord will raise up many to have a heart for this ministry in our society, that they will have *faith* and work diligently to overcome abuse and that healing from abuse miracles will occur in the U.S. and in our world. "Now He did not do many mighty works there because of their unbelief" (Matthew 13:58). By faith, expect miracles from God's mighty works when it comes to victim abuse because God is able to do exceedingly, abundantly above all that we ask or think, according to the power that works in us (Ephesians 3:20)!

My plan is to drop off a copy of *Overcoming Abuse: Embracing Peace Volume I* and *II, Your Encyclopedic Guide to Freedom from Abuse* to a shelter/safe house wherever I travel. Reaching out to a victim can encourage her to change her life. Changing one victim's life can change the next generation—and as a result, generations thereafter can live abuse-free lives! Together you and I can drop-off a copy of *Volume I* to places where we know a victim is likely to receive it. Each one of us can reach out to a victim! Are you worried that you will be judged for assisting a victim through this book? I'm not.

Consider the source and the foundation of that person's judgment first. In this world, those that have a dark, critical spirit and an agenda to negatively review people's approach to problem-solving will exist; they actually thrive on posting negative comments. Consider their personal lineup and the fact that they're not bringing resolution to the problem of abuse. Rather, they're attempting to victimize you for assisting the abused. How about encouraging a victim today instead!

Can you foresee the impact of when victims are notified that there's hope and healing from the trauma of abuse? Can you imagine if each one of us would do victim outreach and encourage a victim about overcoming her abuse what the results would be? Encouraging: it's a chain link of *courage* from God to us and on to others. Victims of abuse—may we meet them where they're at, may we encourage them, may we support them, may we build them up. Be an encourager toward freedom from abuse!

> **"He will redeem their life from oppression and violence."**
>
> - Psalm 72:14 -

LIZ'S STORY

I MET MY FORMER husband, Hank, at a nightclub in New York City, where we had both been raised. I was twenty-two, going to school for Radiology, and working part-time at a hospital. A couple of weeks after we had met, he called, and we began to date regularly. A year later, he proposed. Two years from the day that we met, we married. We were both Christians and had a church wedding. I was born and raised Catholic; I attended Catholic school for twelve years. Hank was raised in the United Pentecostal Church (UPC) because his father was a UPC minister. Hank came from a good family. We married at a non-denominational church because I was no longer practicing Catholicism and he was no longer UPC. At age eighteen, I had become very disillusioned with the Catholic Church, so I stopped all of my participation and church activities there; it was at that time, that I accepted salvation as a Christian.

We were married for seven years, so it was a total of *nine years* invested in this relationship! I have two sons from my marriage to Hank. Hank had four children (two boys and two girls) from a previous marriage; I played a big role in raising them. Up until this day, they still call me for guidance and direction. I had this opportunity to raise his children because he had unlimited visitation rights. So the children would spend lots of time in our home—and I was never opposed to that—I wanted them to visit as much as they wanted to. What I *did not* find out, until I was having marital problems with Hank, was that he had treated his first wife in the same way that he treated me: *very controlling.* And there was infidelity and drinking involved. Hank had completely lied to me!

All Hank gave me as the reason for his divorce was that he suspected that his wife had been unfaithful! Hank initially told me he only had three children and in fact only three children visited him. One day, right before Hank and I got married, the children's grandmother (Hank's mother) called inquiring, "Where's Hank?...he's late for his son's baptism." It was through her that I discovered that Hank had *four* children. Hank said that he had not told me about his youngest son because he did not look like his other son—as he was so fair skinned—and he said it wasn't his son. Hank said that he believed that his wife had had an affair when she conceived him.

I have never believed this is true about his ex-wife and neither does anyone else in the family. It wasn't until our third year of marriage that I was able to include his youngest son along with his other three children to visit in our home. I just finally put my foot down and said, "That's it I am not going to exclude this child anymore!" Hank's ex-wife called to ask if we would watch the children over New Year's. She asked, "All four of them?" I said, "Absolutely!" Hank was *furious* because at that point he had never let the little boy come over to spend time with us.

When I was married to Hank, he refused to allow me to continue to go to college. After the divorce I went back to school and obtained a bachelor's degree in Family Studies with a minor in Government. Hank was not a college graduate, he had taken

LIZ'S STORY

some classes; he was the only one in his family that was not a college graduate. Hank worked as a car salesman. The very first time that I experienced any form of abuse from Hank was actually about a year before we got married; he had been drinking and he slapped me. At that point I gave him an ultimatum, spelling out the guidelines—*if* we were going to get married. I told him that if he continued to drink, I would have to stop seeing him. Hank stopped drinking for year *before* and a year *after* we got married. I *know* now, that it was *not* the drinking that caused him to be abusive.

When Hank started drinking again a year after we were married, I stood by him because I had been raised in a domestic violent family. I believed that even though I had not been able to help my father, I would be able to help Hank with his alcoholism and temper. I was all too familiar with abuse to recognize my overly ambitious plan. I was sexually abused by an uncle as a child, and when my father was drunk, he would verbally and emotionally abuse me. I watched my mother being physically and emotionally abused by my father. This was especially abusive toward my mother and for my siblings and me to watch because my mother was legally blind. Usually my brother and sister, or anyone that disagreed or went against my dad, would end up being physically abused by him; I just never went against him, so I only got the psychological abuse. I got his approval because I was the good child and the high achiever.

I initiated the divorce from my husband when the abuse turned to my children. I had been going to counseling at my church, and the counselor said that our home was not a safe place for the children to be in and suggested that I leave. The *breakthrough* for me came when Hank kicked our two-year-old son. Hank had asked our son to leave the kitchen and when he came back in just to ask me a question Hank kicked him with his boot. It was at *that moment* that *I knew* I needed to leave!

Leaving him had to stay absolutely hidden because he had always threatened me that if I left him, he would kill me. At the time, I worked at a military base. I hired an attorney with money that I had secured from work. Because of my place of employment, I felt very safe there so I did all of the work that I had to do toward the divorce while on base.

I first escaped, temporarily, to my parent's home. When it was time to make the permanent move, my sister came to my house to help me. Unfortunately, Hank showed up as I was leaving. Every time I would put an article of clothing or shoes in the car, he would put them back in the house. However, ironically enough, he respected my sister and she basically told him "Y'all are divorcing and she's leaving." So, he let me drive off with my sister. My sister at the time was involved in an abusive marriage as well, so we became a team. She and I had recognized that we had fallen into the same trap that my mother did. We felt we would be stronger if we worked together and helped each other out. Both of our husbands were *extremely abusive* and *threatening*. I had to take on an extra job because Hank refused to pay child support—as my punishment for leaving. My sister and I purchased a home, we raised our children together, and it became a secure, safe environment for us.

We both went back to school and we would alternate our schedules so one of us would always be available to watch the children. We had amazingly good jobs and we just pulled our resources together to create that safe haven—as opposed to isolating ourselves separately, where our former spouses would have access to us or the children. Our former spouses knew that one of us would always be home and that we would call the police if they showed up, so they learned to just stay away. My mother also became a strong support system. She had already heard the way Hank talked to me and had voiced her disapproval of the way Hank would speak so abusively to me. My mother was confused

LIZ'S STORY

as to why I would continue to stay with him. She had confronted me as to why I would tolerate his verbal abuse; and I had expressed that it was what *she herself* had done in her marriage. My mother reminded me that she was limited in her resources and was also blind; but that I was not. My mother brought to mind that I didn't have liabilities; she pointed out that I had a good job and had the resources to leave. She said that that's what I needed to do. So she became one of my greatest strengths.

Hank and I have been divorced for twenty-two years now. I didn't start dating until about a year and a half after our divorce. About three and a half years after being divorced, I met my current husband, James. We met at the hospital where I was working. James comes from a loving, functional family; however, he too was divorced. James' reason for his divorce was that his ex-wife never cut ties with her family. So many times she was at her parents' home instead of their home; he said this made it very difficult for their marriage to ever develop. James wanted to go to medical school and when he was offered a military scholarship she was *not* encouraging or supportive in that regard *at all*. We dated, fell in love, and got married. James had three sons from his previous marriage; we don't have any children together. James is currently a physician. James and I divorced after eleven years of marriage because of his neglect in disciplining his own children, who had begun dabbling in drugs and alcohol. I was determined that I was not going to allow my two biological children to be raised in that type of environment!

James and I remained divorced for four years and then we reconciled and remarried after his children were grown and out of the home. James is *so different* than Hank; he is totally approving of the things I want to do and encourages what I want to accomplish. James has always been a loving father toward my children. James is not threatened by my education or desire for education or my job; he thoroughly supports me in whatever I want to do which is very unlike Hank. The kind of relationship that James and I have is one of mutual respect for one another. James so values my thoughts, my ideas; when he speaks of me to others, he lifts me up as the most incredible woman that he has ever known. James is the complete opposite of what I experienced in my abusive marriage. This is very special to me because I grew up with family violence. I had *never* experienced observing a husband that is accepting of his wife—being who she is and not just being who he wants her to be.

Even though James and I may think differently on certain situations or issues, he never makes me feel as if my thinking is inferior. It's just different. Many times, he has said that he can learn from me; that would *never ever* have come out of my abusive husband's mouth! In fact, according to Hank I knew *nothing*, I was *stupid*, and I was *uneducated*. In that marriage I was not allowed to do anything outside of the home. Hank was insanely jealous of every relationship that I had; even of my friends. I was very isolated, and as a result, lost all of my friends during that time. James accepts all of my friends and encourages me to have all of those relationships.

I experienced every type of abuse imaginable in my marriage with Hank (in every single aspect) from morning to night. It was a constant degrading and attacking of my self-value or worth and inflating his. Hank controlled our money, what I wore; he controlled everywhere I went (when I wasn't compliant *or* even if I was compliant). When either drugs or alcohol kicked in, it became *very* physical. If I said I was leaving, he would break down and cry and say that he was sorry and would never do it again *or* he would threaten me with my life. Of course, I believed him—I believed his apologies *and* his threats. I wanted to keep our family intact. I gave him another chance, and another chance, and another chance.

The difference in my non-abusive life *now* is that this life has allowed me to pursue my dreams and to go after them! The dreams that I had in my early twenties were completely shattered. With my married life now, I can follow my dreams, get the education I want, and have my own business. I've gone from being a beaten-down woman to a woman who feels that women can indeed have it all, in my opinion. We can't have it all at the same time, but we can follow what we aspire to and get there!

My sons are now young men, and although they don't remember my abusive lifestyle, they understand why our marriage ended in divorce, without even being told. They can tell on their own why the divorce happened, because their dad has never changed. My sons have noticed that their dad does some of the things that he did to me with his current wife; they've figured it out on their own. I think what my past family violence has done for my sons without them remembering or being exposed to it is they have become the *most incredible* fathers! My sons have the most giving spirits; they're helpful and encouraging to their wives. They became determined on their own that their children were not going to have the type of father that they had. Their biological father's absence catapulted them into a desire to be the best that they could for their own children because their father wasn't there for them.

My marriage to James has been a blessing to both my children and my step-children (James' sons), for they have flourished. The structure, boundaries, and discipline that was and continues to be provided for my stepsons empowers them. They recognize that I am not going to *rescue* or *enable* them into destructive behaviors for their lives. They have realized that there's consequences for the bad and praises for the good; this has helped them to *want* to become better men. They feel my love, for I have taken the time to invest in their lives by setting limits and demonstrating my value for them.

As a result of my family having become a blended family, I currently have sixteen grandchildren with two more on the way. Family abuse has made its mark on the grandchildren *only in the form of observation.* The biological grandchildren of my former abusive spouse (Hank) understand why the divorce happened, and to some degree, even though they love their grandfather, there's somewhat of a lack of admiration and respect for him at times. They notice the way he cares for himself (which is not very good) and the way that he cares for his wife (their stepgrandma), they understand that he's not the man that he could be. However, my grandchildren are functioning, healthy, and thriving because the cycle of family violence has stopped for our current family.

My past abusive relationship was toxic, unhealthy, and destructive. My abusive lifestyle was more than challenging, it was painfully difficult. My abuse-free life now is fulfilling, hopeful, and satisfying. If I could change having ended up in an abusive marriage, I would have dated for a longer period of time to really comprehend that it was not the alcohol that was making him abusive. I would have requested that we have some pre-marital counseling which would have perhaps alerted me to some red flags. In that counseling, I would have liked to have gained awareness and insight into how my own father's alcoholism was playing into my ending up in an abusive relationship. I would have wanted for the counseling to bring out what I was to look for as far as me not continuing in my abusive cycle. I would have liked to have obtained the tools in order to know what to identify in men, so as not to fall into the same family violence trap that my mother fell into. Of course, not having married my abusive spouse is a Catch-22 because if I hadn't married him, then I wouldn't have the amazing sons and the marvelous grandchildren that I have!

I'm so grateful that there are so many more resources available to abused women these days compared to when I was in the midst of my abusive cycle. Part of what I do now in my practice as a Mediator is connecting abused women to those resources that they need. A victim comes out of an abuse shell, and when she does, she is *limitless* with opportunities—that is, when someone is no longer controlling her life. After my divorce from my abusive husband (even as a single mother) I ran for City Council—where I was able to serve—and eventually served as mayor.

This was not new; these were things I had always wanted to do but I was stifled in my abusive marriage. I think that under the abuse I lived a very fearful life, so when challenges began to present themselves while I was under the duress of fear, I managed to let fear stifle me. The fear made me think that I wasn't equipped to fulfill my dreams. Ultimately, I had to recognize that God does not guide us where He doesn't provide for us!

So, God truly made me realize the lies that I had been told by my father, my abusive uncle, and former husband. He helped me to see that He had equipped me with *every* single thing that I needed to do—with *everything* that He had purposed for me to do! Now that I look to God as my leader, so many doors have been opened and I've been allowed to go through them. I am so grateful because I could have lost that opportunity! This, in turn, has helped my children and grandchildren to see that they can do the same. It is a huge testimony that I don't ever want to be the victim anymore—the victim has no purpose. If we can overcome our own victimization with God's help and look to Him for healing, He will take us down paths that we have never dreamed of—far above what we've ever dreamed of.

He'll restore the years that were lost, we just need to pull ourselves up by our bootstraps; look to God and let Him be our *All*. I want to be about God's work and do my best, and I can't fulfill

His purpose while in an abusive cycle. God gives us a future that we never would have expected on our own.

Truly, a victim is not trapped—there are lots of opportunities in existence. While it seems incredibly difficult being captive, there's so much out there for the victim, with many men and women willing to help through the process. Even if a victim is afraid, she has to do it *afraid*; *because* leaving the abusive relationship is so amazing for her and her family! There is *nothing* to fear except staying in the *same abuse*. A victim has to take that leap of faith and jump because God has so much more for her than where she's at!

ENDNOTES

PART I
AMERICA'S HISTORY OF ABUSE

1. R. Emerson Dobash and Russell P. Dobash, *Violence Against Wives* (New York: The Free Press, 1979) 37-38.

2. Julia O'Faolain and Lauro Martines (eds.) *Not in God's Image: Women in History* (Glasgow: Fontana/Collins, 1974) 53-56, 63, 67-69.

3. John J. Macionis, *Sociology: Annotated Instructor's Edition, 10th ed.* (New Jersey: Pearson/Prentice Hall, 2005) 325.

4. Karl Menninger, M.D. *Whatever Became of SIN?* (New York: Hawthorn Books, Inc., 1973) 14.

5. Thomas Aquinas, *Summa Theologica* (New York: Benziger Brothers, 1947) II-II, Q. 26, Art. 10.

6. Julia O'Faolain and Lauro Martines (eds.) *Not in God's Image: Women in History from the Greeks to the Victorians*, (New York: Harper and Row, 1973) 196-197.

PART II
RECONCILIATION ADVISOR VS. THE PROFESSIONAL

7. J. Fagan, and S. Wexler, "Crime at Home and in the Streets: The Relationship Between Family and Stranger Violence," *Violence and Victims* 2, no. 1 (Spring, 1987) 5-23.

8. American Psychological Association, *Violence and the Family: Report of the American Psychological Association Presidential Task Force on Violence and the Family* (Washington, D.C.: American Psychological Association, 1996) 10.

RESOURCES

The National Domestic Violence Hotline
1-800-799-7233 1-800-799-SAFE Toll-Free
www.ndvh.org
www.thehotline.org

Domestic Shelters
Free national database of domestic violence shelter programs.
www.domesticshelters.org

Break the Cycle
202-824-0707
www.breakthecycle.org

Break the Silence (BTSADV)
1-800-855-BTS (1777)
Mon-Sun. Supportive assistance and connection to resources.
www.breakthesilencedv.org

Final Salute, Inc.
Mission: To provide homeless women Veterans with safe and suitable housing.
One of the factors contributing to female veteran homelessness is domestic violence.
703-224-8845
https://www.finalsaluteinc.org

Military OneSource
800-342-9647 (U.S. or Overseas)
TTY/TDD: Dial 711 and give the toll-free number 800-342-9647
https://www.militaryonesource.mil/
 24/7/365 abuse helpline via telephone or on website, click on Confidential Help in the menu; live chat with a prompt response is available for all electronic devices.
To locate resources at your military installation go to:
https://installations.militaryonesource.mil/

Women's Law
www.womenslaw.org
Provides civilian and military domestic violence information and laws.

National Military Family Association
2800 Eisenhower Avenue, Suite 250
Alexandria, VA 22314
703-931-6632
info@MilitaryFamily.org

Operation We are Here
Resource Center for the Military & its Supporters
Email: opwearehere@gmail.com
www.operationwearehere.com

The Mary Kay Foundation for Domestic Abuse
Mary Kay sponsored text-for-help line (for victim or if you know a victim that needs help).
Text "loveis" to 22522

HOPE for the Heart Care Center
Prayer & Christian Counseling referral source.
Hope care representatives are available M-F 24 hrs.
1-800-488-4673 1-800-488- HOPE 4673 Toll-Free

RESOURCES

Americans Overseas Domestic Violence Crisis Center
International Toll-Free (24/7)
1-866-USWOMEN 1-866-879-6636 Toll-Free
www.866uswomen.org

National Teen Dating Abuse Helpline
1-866-331-9474 Toll-Free
www.loveisrespect.org

Childhelp USA/National Child Abuse Hotline
1-800-422-4453 1-800-4-A-CHILD Toll-Free
www.childhelpusa.org www.childhelp.org

World Childhood Foundation Inc.
Mission: To stimulate, promote and enable the development of solutions to prevent and address sexual abuse, exploitation, and violence against children.
900 3rd Ave. 29th Floor
New York, NY 10022
212-867-6088
Website:info@childhood-USA.org

Rape, Abuse, & Incest National Network
1-800- 656-4673 1-800-656- HOPE Toll-Free
www.rainn.org

National Human Trafficking Resource Center/Polaris Project
Call: 1-888-373-7888 Toll-Free Text: HELP to Be Free (233733)
www.polarisproject.org

Battered Women's Justice Project
1-800-903-0111
www.bwjp.org

Brain Injury Resource Center
P.O.BOX 84151
Seattle, WA 98124-5451
206-621-8558
Email: %20brain@headinjury.com
www.headinjury.com

Deaf Abused Women's Network (DAWN)
One in two deaf women experience family violence.
One in three deaf women is a victim of sexual assault.
Email: Hotline@deafdawn.org
VP: 202-559-5366
www.deafdawn.org

Abused Deaf Women's Advocacy Services (ADWAS)
Email: Deafhelp@thehotline.org
VP: 1-855-812-1000 Toll-Free

American Bar Association Commission on Domestic Violence
1-202-662-1000
www.abanet.org/domviol

ASPIRE News
An app that is hidden in a traditional news reader icon with cryptic programming capability.
Smartphone App Offers Resource Contacts & Help for Victims of Abuse: The victim can program the app to alert "trusted personal contacts/resources" of the victim's emergency status.
https://www.whengeorgiasmiled.org/the-aspire-news-app/

RESOURCES

NNEDV
National Network to End Domestic Violence
1325 Massachusetts Ave NW 7th Floor
Washington, DC 20005-4188
202-543-5566
www.techsafety.org

In order to maintain victim safety and privacy through the proper software, The National Network to End Domestic Violence (NNEDV) Safety Net Project, together with the Office for Victims of Crime, Office of Justice Programs, U.S. Department of Justice provide guidance on a Digital Services Toolkit to protect victims from digital abuse. The toolkit is equipped with resources for local programs that offer services via text, chat, video call, and other digital technologies.

TracFone Wireless, Inc.
A pre-paid mobile phone network operating in the U.S., Puerto Rico, and the U.S. Virgin Islands, who also offers several other cellphone brands with services from various phone companies. Monday-Sunday 8:00 a.m.-11:45 p.m. Eastern Standard Time 1-800-867-7183 0r 1-880-378-9575 Press # 4 then repeatedly ask for customer service when the prompts do not apply to you. If the prompts ask for your TracFone # or other information which you do not have, say "other" and a representative will answer.
www.tracfone.com

RESOURCES

WOMAN ABUSE SCREENING TOOL* (WAST)

1. In general, how would you describe your relationship?
   - ☐ a lot of tension
   - ☐ some tension
   - ☐ no tension

2. Do you and your partner work out arguments with:
   - ☐ great difficulty
   - ☐ some difficulty
   - ☐ no difficulty

3. Do arguments ever result in you feeling down or bad about yourself?
   - ☐ often
   - ☐ sometimes
   - ☐ never

4. Do arguments ever result in hitting, kicking, or pushing?
   - ☐ often
   - ☐ sometimes
   - ☐ never

5. Do you ever feel frightened by what your partner says or does?
   - ☐ often
   - ☐ sometimes
   - ☐ never

6. Has your partner ever abused you physically?
   - ☐ often
   - ☐ sometimes
   - ☐ never

7. Has your partner ever abused you emotionally?
   - ☐ often
   - ☐ sometimes
   - ☐ never

8. Has your partner ever abused you sexually?
   - ☐ often
   - ☐ sometimes
   - ☐ never

---

*Source: Brown, J., Lent, B., Schmidt, G., & Sas, S. (2000). Application of the Woman Abuse Screening Tool (WAST) and WAST-short in the family practice setting. *Journal of Family Practice, 49,* 896-903.

OVERCOMING ABUSE VOLUME III

Adult Victim Domestic Violence Assessment Tool

Client Name: _____ Date: _____ Worker: _____

Partner Name: _____ Relationship: _____ ☐ Current ☐ Past

PROMPT: The next few questions can be uncomfortable for some people. I do have to ask them in order to better understand if there is danger and how much. Again, these may or may not pertain to you.

		PAST		Last 60 Days?		NOTES
	Assesses patterns, frequency, and whether the victim faces a continuing threat of danger from the abusive partner					
	Has your (abusive) partner:	No	Yes	No	Yes	
Risk of Danger	Prevented you from: working/school/church/friends/family?					
	Confined you against your will? (blocked exits, lock door, hide keys)					
	Listened to your phone calls or violated your privacy? (e.g. check text messages/emails, requires your passwords, etc.)					
	Taken/broken your telephone, turned off your service, or kept you from calling for help? *					
	Does your partner control your access to money? Coerced you to give or stolen your money?					
	Called you degrading names or emotionally insulted you? Humiliated you at home or in public? (emotional abuse)					
	Has your partner stalked, followed you, constantly harassed or texted/emailed you? * (Threats of physical or emotional harm)					
	Caused fear for your safety/Threatened to kill you? * (What do you think, fear your partner might do?)					
	Forced you to use drugs? Drugged you without your knowledge?					
	Exhibited reckless behavior? Behaved violently in public? (e.g. driven too fast with you and/or children in the car)					
	Damaged property (don locks in walls, broken furniture, destroyed your possessions)					
	Follow/Stalked or Threatened to take the children?					
	Caused you to fear for the safety of your children or harmed the children? Threatened to kill the children? *					
	Been on probation, parole, or served a time of imprisonment in relation to offenses of violence or sexual assault?					
	Is there anything else that you believe is a threat or serious threat to your safety and/or the children?					

		PAST		Last 60 Days?		NOTES
	If violence is present in the family, assess for severity and potential lethality					
	Has your (abusive) partner:	No	Yes	No	Yes	
Assessing Lethality	Threatened to use or has used a gun or weapon? Owns a gun/weapon or can get one easily? **					
	Ever choked, strangled or suffocated you or attempted? **					
	Ever disagreed or had control over sexual issues? Ever forced you to have sex? *					
	Ever touched you sexually against your will or without your consent? * (Prompt: if you say "no", intimate because you were afraid?)					
	Pressured you to engage in pornography, fantasies or have sex with others? *					

RESOURCES

		Last 60 Days?		NOTES
Identifies whether or not you should be concerned about the abusive partner causing great harm, destruction or death. An endorsement of YES to any of the following statements indicates increased risk of danger.				
Has your (abusive) partner:	No	Yes	No	Yes
Hurt you during your pregnancy?				
Hit, slapped, kicked, bit, punch, cut, or burned you?*				
Have you experienced any physical injuries caused by the abuse? What was the degree of severity of the injuries?**				
Escalated violence or controlling behaviors; becoming worse or more frequent?				
Has your partner ever harmed or killed a family pet or threatened to do so?				
Have you experienced homelessness due to domestic violence or sexual assault?				
Cause any conflict regarding child contact or residency issues and/or current Family Court proceedings?				
Has Child Protective Services been called related to the domestic abuse?**				
If yes, what is the current status/outcome of the case? **				

Section label: Assessing Legal Options and Referral

*If physical violence or threats of physical violence occurred within the last 60 days & there is risk of continued violence without intervention, discuss the option of a **PROTECTIVE ORDER**. Complete the application **BEFORE** the intake ends.

☐ Check here if a Protective Order was discussed. Was client connected with advocacy? _____

** If the client experienced Felony level assault (use of a weapon, severe bodily injury, or Sexual Assault) or CPS involvement due to DV, refer to the High Risk Advocate.

☐ Check here if client was referred to the High Risk Advocate.

Has/Is your (abusive) partner:	No	Yes	NOTES
Threatened or attempted suicide/ or injured self intentionally?			
Been arrested for other violent crimes?			
Used drugs or alcohol?			
Had a protective order against him/her?			
Unemployed?			
Had a history of mental illness? (including undiagnosed conditions)			

Section label: Abuser Information

Have You:	No	Yes	NOTES
Left/ fled the home because of the abuse?			
Accessed a domestic violence agency before today?			
Called the Police?***			
If yes, how many times? _____ Was there ever an arrest? _____ When? _____ Where? _____			
Filed for a protective order?***			
If yes, when? _____ Did you receive one? _____ If yes, what county/ State? _____			
Other Interventions or protective actions?			

Section label: Use of Intervention

***If there has been a police report for family violence or a protective order, there is potential for Crime Victims' Compensation

☐ Check here if CVC was discussed. Was client referred to advocacy? _____

243

OVERCOMING ABUSE VOLUME III

SAMPLE TECHNOLOGY ABUSE LOG

NNEDV

Information About the Abuser	
Name of the person abusing or stalking you.	
Relationship of that person to you (if relevant).	
Contact information of that person	
Home address	Work address
Phone number(s)	Email address(es)
Online account(s), including screen name & type of online account (facebook, etc.)	
Other information about the abuser (that might be relevant)	

Description of the Abuse	
Date:	Time:
Describe the event:	
Type of technology involved:	
Were there any witnesses? What are their names?	

Documentation
If you were able to document the abuse, what type of documentation do you have?

Other Information
Did you report it to the police? If so, what is the report number and officer name?
Did you go to the hospital/see a doctor? If so, what was the hospital/doctor name?

Sample Technology Abuse Log ©2014 National Network to End Domestic Violence, Safety Net Project • TechSafety.org Supported by US DOJ-OVC Grant # 2011-VF-GX-K016. Opinions, findings, and conclusions or recommendations expressed are the authors and do not necessarily represent the views of DOJ.

Using the HELPS Tool with Women Seeking Domestic Violence Services*

IN THE CASE OF domestic violence, women should be asked about various forms of physical abuse that could lead to a brain injury. Advocates and program staff are encouraged to utilize the following checklist, which parallels the categories of the HELPS, to aid in determining if women entering into programs should be seen by a doctor for further evaluation.

____ Did your partner ever Hit you in the face or head? With what?
____ Did your partner ever slam your head into a wall or another object, or push you so that you fell and hit your head?
____ Did your partner ever shake you?
____ Did your partner ever try to strangle or choke you, or do anything else that made it hard for you to breathe?
____ Did you ever go to the Emergency room after an incident? Why?
____ Did they ask you whether you had been hit on the head or indicate that they suspected a head injury or concussion?
____ Was there ever a time when you thought you needed to go to the ER, but didn't go because you couldn't afford it or your partner prevented you?

____ If you did go to the ER, do you think you got all the treatment you needed?

____ Did you ever Lose consciousness or black out as a result of what your partner did to you?

____ Have you been having Problems concentrating or remembering things? Are you having trouble finishing things you start to do?

____ Are people telling you that you don't seem like yourself, or that your behavior has changed?

____ Does your partner say you have changed, and use that as an excuse to abuse you?

____ Have you been having difficulty performing your usual activities?

____ Are you experiencing mood swings that you don't understand?

____ Has it gotten harder for you to function when you are under stress?

____ Have you been Sick or had any physical problems? What kind?

____ Do you experience any reoccurring headaches or fatigue?

____ Have you experienced any changes in your vision, hearing, or sense of smell or taste?

____ Do you find yourself dizzy or experiencing a lack of balance?

*Reprinted with permission of the Empire Justice Center, Building Bridges: A Cross-Systems Training Manual for Domestic Violence Programs and Disability Service Providers in New York, 2006

HELPS Screening Tool for Traumatic Brain Injury**

Directions: Score 1 point for every question answered 'Yes'. A score of 2 or more, particularly if the injury affects function (P), should be considered as a sign of a possible injury that needs to be further explored with a more extensive interview and medical or neuropsychological work-up.

HELPS Screening Tool for Traumatic Brain Injury**

Question	No	Yes	Comments
H = Did you ever hit your head? Were you ever hit on your head?			
E = Were you ever seen in an emergency room by a doctor or hospitalized? If so, for what reason?			
L = Did you ever lose consciousness? For how long? For what reason?			
P = Did you have any problems after you were hit on the head?			
- Headaches			
- Dizziness			
- Anxiety			
- Depression			
- Difficulty concentrating			
- Difficulty remembering			
- Difficulty reading, writing, calculating			
- Difficulty performing your old job or school work			
- Changes in behavior or attitude			
- Difficulty problem solving			
- Changes in relationships			
S = Did you have any significant sicknesses after having your head hit?			

** Adapted with permission from the International Center for the Disabled, HELPS Screening Tool, 1992.

OTHER BOOKS BY REINA DAVISON

Overcoming Abuse: Embracing Peace Volume I Your Encyclopedic Guide to Freedom from Abuse arms victims and their support system with a body of knowledge on the trauma of abuse. Victim abuse has historically and up to the present been treated as a mere societal botheration and remains predominantly an unapproachable enigma. Problem-solving clinical faith-based strategies are provided for victims and our society in order that they may experience abuse-free lives. Self-told testimonial stories of triumphant victims that have overcome their abuse are revealed; as the victim is guided to overcome her own abuse. The result: As an overcomer of her abuse—she embraces peace and becomes— the woman God intended her to be! To bring the message of *Overcoming Abuse: Embracing Peace Volume I* to your organization, church, or event, visit: **www.overcomingabuse.info**

Overcoming Abuse: Embracing Peace Volume II Your Encyclopedic Guide to Freedom from Abuse uses a holistic approach to guide the victim: which includes a renewed attitude, overcomer principles, and techniques for permanently removing their self from an unsafe abusive relationship. The victim gains lifetime clinical and faith-based solution skills, to heal from the trauma of abuse. She learns to stop her abuse and chooses—a curated lifestyle of peace. Surrendering her victimization and accepting her overcomer role is the precursor to a victim's willingness and ability to experience an abuse-free life (that is infilled with peace). A plan of action and a blueprint is laid out for the victim, her support system and society; to maneuver the healing, prevention, and stopping of victim trauma and family abuse.

To bring the message of ***Overcoming Abuse: Embracing Peace Volume II*** to your organization, church, or event, visit: **www.overcomingabuse.info**

OTHER BOOKS BY REINA DAVISON

Overcoming Abuse: Child Sexual Abuse Prevention and Protection: A Guide for Parents Caregivers and Helpers is a parent's handbook to learn the dynamics of Child Sexual Abuse (CSA), the sex offender profile, and *how* to prevent and protect a child from being a target of CSA anywhere, including the internet. This book guides the adult on initiating conversation to help the child gain an understanding about the precious gift of his body; and walks the adult through introducing a healthy, age-appropriate, biblical perspective on human sexuality. The concept of overcoming Child Sexual Abuse is fully addressed to encourage and strengthen the parent/caregiver and child as they come together to empower the child against CSA (whether he/she has never experienced CSA or has already been a target).

To bring the message of *Overcoming Abuse: Child Sexual Abuse Prevention and Protection* to your organization, church, or event, visit: **www.overcomingabuse.info**

Overcoming Abuse: My Body Belongs to God and Me A Child's Body Safety Guide is a book written for a parent, caregiver, or helper to read to children from pre-school to fifth grade. Trusted adults can teach children how to identify *no touch people* and how to distinguish "good touch" (God touch) from "no touch" in a non-frightening way and non-threatening environment. A series of possible scenarios with no touch people (including the internet) are presented, and the child is guided as to how to respond in a similar situation. The child is emboldened to stay away from no touch people and is strengthened and encouraged that most touch *is* good touch!

To bring the message of **Overcoming Abuse: My Body Belongs to God and Me** to your organization, church, or event, visit: **www.overcomingabuse.info**

www.ingramcontent.com/pod-product-compliance
Lightning Source LLC
Chambersburg PA
CBHW071112160426
43196CB00013B/2542